D1593643

# THE HIGH SCHOOL ADOLESCENT

# THE HIGH SCHOOL

MORRIS A. SKLANSKY, M.D.
SYLVIA W. SILVERMAN
HELEN G. RABICHOW

Association Press

# ADOLESCENT

*Understanding and Treating
His Emotional Problems*

710623

New York

The High School Adolescent

Copyright © 1969 by Association Press

SBN: Hardbound edition 8096–1755–2

Library of Congress catalog card number: 70-90343

 72

Printed in the United States of America

# Preface

SCHOLARSHIP AND GUIDANCE ASSOCIATION is a voluntary, non-sectarian, interracial social agency serving emotionally disturbed adolescents, ages thirteen-eighteen, and their parents since 1911.

Referrals are made to the Agency by the Board of Education and its various departments and personnel, and by other agencies in the community including family, child welfare, clinics, hospitals, settlement houses, courts.

The Agency serves the Chicago Metropolitan Community and the clientele represents a cross-section of the various social, economic, racial, ethnic and religious strata of the community. The caseload has averaged about forty per cent non-white (Negro, Oriental, Puerto Rican, Mexican). Adolescents whose families receive public assistance or who live on marginal incomes (about one-third of the caseload and include white and non-white) receive free service, and in addition, such adolescents are eligible for monthly scholarship assistance for expenses incidental to high school attendance. Where family income is above the marginal level fees are charged, based on a sliding scale according to the family's ability to pay. All service includes work with the parents as well as with the adolescent.

The material in this book evolves out of more than fifteen years of case discussions in seminars and staffings with Dr. M. A. Sklansky, our psychiatric consultant. It represents a distillation

7

of theory and practice as this applies to helping the high school adolescent with his emotional problems which hamper normal growth toward maturity.

While the Agency also uses the helping technique of group treatment, this book deals with the adolescent in a one-to-one relationship. If the goal of work with the adolescent has a therapeutic intent, it is basic to begin with an understanding of the uniqueness of the adolescent personality, his special needs and problems, his characteristic ways of behaving and relating. Out of such understanding appropriate, differential and flexible application of therapeutic techniques can be implemented in whatever particular process or method is employed.

To suggest that there is one solution, one way of dealing with the problems which adolescents present is a gross oversimplification of the human condition. We are aware that there are many approaches and a variety of techniques in work with the adolescent. This book, however, is not intended to survey the total range of methodologies. Rather, proceeding from the base of psychoanalytic theory, we perceive the adolescent as an individual personality living in a social and cultural milieu where both internal and external factors impinge on him. To help the adolescent in his developmental struggles, it is essential to understand the interrelationship of cultural forces and the adolescent's needs and personal conflicts.

Young people are particularly attuned to the defects, the paradoxes, the discontents of the world in which they live. In a period of explosive changes these become even more apparent to them. Especially important today is the paradox of poverty and discrimination in a society of affluence. The individual who is victimized by virtue of race, color or creed and deprived of equal opportunities for the economic, educational, employment, and social advantages available to the majority is handicapped also in his personality development. Such inequities which damage, degrade, and warp human beings must be eradicated by massive social measures, for only within a society which allows equal opportunities for all its members and respects differences can people be free to develop their human potentials and their personalities to the fullest. This must be a major goal of a humanistic society.

But regardless of the world in which he lives, the basic internal aspects of the psychology of the adolescent, as is true of human nature generally, have remained essentially the same throughout the ages. Cultural changes far outpace the lagging adaptations of the personality. The adolescent period, visualized as a phase of striving for the attainment of adult status, produces similar experiences for all youth in all cultures, in all environments. We have found that the need of the adolescent for meaningful human relationships, for understanding and help in growing up cuts across color, creed, economic, social and ethnic barriers. While the capacity to articulate is a general requisite in any helping process, there are many different ways of communicating universal needs. It is the responsibility of the professional helping person to be sensitive to and understand not only the direct verbalizations of the adolescent, but also the non-verbal, the unexpressed communications, the feelings which reveal underlying needs. Out of such understanding he can help the troubled individual move toward making appropriate change.

Our endeavors are directed toward working with the adolescent in his total environment. Our goal is to strengthen the adolescent's ego and his adaptive defenses so that he suffers less from disabling inner conflicts and is freer to use his energies in coping with and changing the external environment within the limits of his ability.

We use the term counselor in a broad sense intended to include persons with training and experience from various disciplines who are working with adolescents in a professional role with the goal of helping them to deal with their problems more constructively. Over the years we have given and participated in workshops, seminars, lectures, as well as provided consultative services to educators, guidance counselors, employment counselors, seminarians, and social workers. These professional people found our approach in working with adolescents relevant and useful to them in their own disciplines and settings. We hope that those who read this book will also find the material helpful.

MORRIS A. SKLANSKY, M.D.
SYLVIA W. SILVERMAN
HELEN G. RABICHOW

# Acknowledgments

THE AUTHORS wish to acknowledge their gratitude and appreciation to: The Wieboldt Foundation of Chicago for their generous grant which financed the writing of this book; the Agency's staff for their interest and dedication to helping the disturbed high school adolescent; the progressive, enlightened Board of Directors who support Agency services to adolescents in need of help.

Special acknowledgment is due Charlotte Towle, Professor Emeritus, University of Chicago, School of Social Service Administration, who came to the Agency upon her retirement in 1964 and worked in a consultative capacity and student training until shortly before her death in 1966. She contributed to us her wisdom, perspective, knowledge and humanity, and encouraged us in our endeavors.

# Contents

# Contents

# THE HIGH SCHOOL ADOLESCENT

# 1

# The Turmoil of Adolescence

THE YOUNG ADOLESCENT is confused and confusing. His life is a mass of contradictions. He is eager and full of hope, yet anxious and fearful. He is still financially and emotionally dependent but one of his major struggles is for independence. He has passed the time when parental protectiveness is welcome, yet he has not reached the point where he is competent to function on his own. His sexual drives are strong but society and his conscience ordinarily restrain him from sexual gratification. He needs and wants help from a concerned adult as he strives for entrance into the adult world yet he will rebel against adult intervention. In his struggle for equilibrium he may act like a small child at one moment, show maturity beyond his years at another, and at the same time that he acts like a small child he may demand the right to be treated like an adult. These contradictions lie in the adolescent process itself.

Adolescent behavior is primarily the result of internal, not external, causes. Every stage in human growth involves its own special tasks. At most age levels the struggles toward the developmental goals are recognized as steps toward achievement. The infant is not blamed for falling when he attempts to stand. But too often, the adolescent struggles are mistaken for permanent willful refusals to adapt to the expectations of the adult world. Most adults, repressing the memory of their own adolescence, find adolescents irritating and troublesome.

Anyone who is attempting to work with adolescents, whether in mass programs for cultural enrichment, vocational and educational motivation and training, neighborhood centers, school or employment counseling, churches, treatment groups, or individually in one to one relationship, needs a basic understanding of the characteristics of the adolescent personality. The behavior which arises out of the adolescent growth process is confusing and inconsistent, but it is a normal manifestation of the process and should be differentiated from the problems and behavior of adolescents with emotional disorders.

The adolescent needs help in dealing with environmental reality and he can be helped to improve his functioning without acquiring insight into his own unconscious processes. The helping person may be a social worker, teacher, guidance or employment counselor, psychiatrist, psychologist, minister or sociologist. Whatever his profession or his specific helping role, his effectiveness will be increased as he acquires insight into the dynamic process of human growth and development, with special understanding of the adolescent personality.

Starting some time between the ages of twelve and fourteen, in most instances, and continuing for almost a decade, human beings undergo sudden changes, internal and external. Within the conscious experience of any individual, the emotional and behavioral upheavals that occur in adolescence are greater than for any other period of life. Stress occurs in other phases of human growth but without the unique combination of physical, psychological, environmental, social and cultural factors which characterizes the adolescent period.

Rapid growth and rapid changes take place from birth and infancy through the childhood years but ordinarily without great environmental pressures and expectations. The school child has settled on certain patterns of adaptation that usually are characteristic of his immediate family and his relatively limited world of school and friends. At pubescence, however, this stability is overthrown by hormonal alteration and the accompanying physiological and psychological changes.

When this change occurs, especially in those hormones relating to sexual reproduction and bodily growth, the whole personality is shaken. The libidinal drive becomes intensified and psychological matters which before were simple and innocuous become complex and charged with strong emotion. Sexual attraction begins to exert strong pull and longing for sexual satisfactions increases. Passions are more intense, longings more urgent, sensitivities are keener, experiences more vivid, and suffering from loss, rejection, shame and guilt is more acute during adolescence than at any time before or after.

The intensification of impulse life clamors at the ego of the adolescent. The defenses he formerly used, which were suitable earlier in his life, no longer function adequately. The ego is in jeopardy. In the process of development, no child escapes completely from anxieties and guilt, and whatever conflict he previously experienced does not disappear at puberty. Earlier conflicts continue and, in addition, with the onset of adolescence, the impulses become more intense and conflicts about these impulses emerge.

The physiological changes are the cause of the typical adolescent reactions. Varying degrees of physiological maturation make a readily observable difference between adolescents in the same environment. The differences in personality and behavior between a fifteen-year-old boy who is still childlike in size and appearance are easily discernible from that of another boy of the same age with a bass voice and sprouting beard.

A rich fantasy life, strong feelings, and action in easy response to impulse are characteristics associated with adolescence, although not all adolescents are alike in these respects. Some are extremely inhibited in both action and fantasy. Others fantasy and feel a great deal but inhibit action. There are adolescents with shallow fantasies who engage in a great deal of acting out. The more usual adolescent has fantasies, acts on impulse to a degree but also is capable of inhibiting actions.

Adolescence coincides approximately with the second decade of life. But ten years is a long time and the early adolescent is different in many ways from one of nineteen. The adolescent period may be divided into three phases, early, middle and late, with observable differences in the personality in each of these phases. The outstanding differences, most important for treatment, are the significance and quality of relationships and the capacity for self-observation.

In the early phase of adolescence there is a tendency to regress to infantile needs and childlike ways of relating. The adolescent seems to give up some of the attainments he achieved earlier. He may become more dependent, demanding and slovenly. He wants freedom to go his own way, but even the demand for independence is reminiscent of the three-year-old shouting, "I want to do it myself," with disregard for reality, compromise and consequences. His tendency is to act to gratify impulse; he has little inclination during this phase to observe himself or to reveal himself to others, especially adults. This behavior can be understood as a regressive defense against the first inner perception of intensified sexual impulse.

In middle adolescence the genital impulses increase in intensity, propelling the progression toward heterosexuality. There may still be infantile relationships, both dependent and transient homosexual ones, but these begin to yield to concern with the opposite sex. Both boys and girls pay more attention to grooming, cleanliness and appearance, and show more than the earlier teasing interest in each other. The adolescent now begins to be interested in the workings of his psyche, but he is still more interested in action and in finding gratification for his impulses. He is distrustful of adults and reveals himself more readily to his peers than to his parents or other adults.

The late adolescent, keenly interested in his heterosexual relationships, is also very much concerned about himself, his self-image, his vocational aims, his future and the meaning of his life. He is observant both of himself and of the world about him. When well-motivated, he is involved and self-examining in any form of psychological treatment.

Throughout the various phases of adolescence there are some developmental differences between boys and girls. Girls usually develop physically earlier than boys, and boys remain in the early adolescent stage for a longer time than girls.

The sexual behavior of boys in early and middle adolescence sometimes resembles the exhibitionistic phase of the four to five-year-old. The object of the sexual impulse is of less importance than competition with other boys and showing off. When sexual intercourse does take place, the partner is of little importance; the sexual act is much like masturbation, self-involved. At this period boys engage in a good deal of sexual talk but less action.

Girls fall in love more readily than boys and they attach importance to being loved by a special boy. With girls the sexual impulses seem secondary to the need for love and tenderness in the relationship. The sexual behavior that occurs may be based on a need to "hold" an individual boy or to comply with the mores of a special group situation rather than for genital satisfaction.

In the covert homosexual relationships of early adolescence there is also a difference between boys and girls. Girls have a tendency to want a one-to-one relationship while boys seek out peer groups. They enjoy the physical contacts of team sports, for example, although both types of relating occur in both sexes. The close relationship with one other girl, the crush girls frequently develop, while it has a somewhat homosexual flavor, is often actually a kind of preparation for heterosexual relationships. During this phase girls discuss sexuality with each other and many girls have an imaginary kind of relationship with males, as with a movie star or popular singer.

In late adolescence girls have a more serious struggle trying to settle their life plans between career and marriage. Even girls with superior talents and opportunities find themselves torn. On the one hand the current emphasis on female equality and their own ambitions press them to develop themselves academically and vocationally. On the other hand their female physiology, the longings for love, heterosexual relationships and children push them toward marriage.

For the development of a healthy mature personality in adulthood, the adolescent must accomplish a number of major integrative tasks during the period of adolescence.

## EMANCIPATION

A basic and continual task during adolescence is the struggle between the wish for dependence and the push toward independence. In order to reach maturity the shift to independence must occur. The direction of a small child's life is set by his parents. The adolescent must strive toward the goal of achieving independent responsibility for management of his own life.

## SEXUALITY

The child normally establishes his sexual identity in a relatively unquestioning identification with the parent of the same sex during the period of quiescence of sexual drives. The adolescent, under pressure, finds his sexual identity diffused. He must redefine his sexual role with the ultimate goal of heterosexual maturation. The libidinal attachment to the parents and the conflicts regarding them which exist in childhood must be resolved. All adolescents must overcome the earlier internal barriers to heterosexuality.

## RELATIONSHIPS

Relationships are defined for the child by the roles he has accepted from his family, school and immediate environment. The adolescent must give up the childish need for his parents and accept himself as different in some ways from his family. The goal is the development of the capacity for mature and stable relationships outside the family.

## CHARACTER FORMATION

The child's personality is consistent with the limits of his small world. He mimics or even caricatures the adults who are close to him and he is what is expected of him by his family and his environment. His ego functions rigidly and with constraint in terms of narrow concepts of reality. He is dependent on gratification from the outside. His superego is essentially parental, not totally internalized, but vigorously defended. Sexual impulses are mainly repressed although aggressive impulses are not so easily managed.

With adolescence comes a loosening of the former ego-superego integration. Earlier conflicts, formerly repressed, revive, are re-expressed and need to be re-resolved in a search for a reintegration. The goal is a more stable character formation with an integrated personality, adaptive ego functioning, mature ego management of impulse and a consistent internalized superego.

## IDENTITY

The child has an adequate but limited sense of self influenced by external definitions. He sees himself as others have chosen to identify him. At the onset of adolescence important aspects of this identity come to be questioned. The adolescent throws himself into his peer group to hold on to some consistent sense of identity. The group values become his values and he fears being different. During the adolescent years his task is to lose his dependence on peer identity, and to develop an adequate sense of the uniqueness of himself as an individual.

## ORIENTATION TOWARD THE FUTURE

The aims of the child are settled for him for the most part by his family and school, accepted without deep personal involvement and with little genuine significance. The adolescent has to shift his sights from the present to the future. In high school education assumes new importance in terms of the formulation of ultimate vocational goals; the selection of friends and activities begins to take on a more directed shape. A mature young adult should have a relatively definite plan for himself about education, career and marriage, and should know his role in respect to his family and his community.

These goals should be attained by the end of adolescence. The psychic health of an adolescent can be appraised in relation to where he stands and how much progress he has made toward the eventual integration of these major developmental tasks.

Many outside factors create stress for the adolescent at the same time that the intense libidinal forces create pressures from within.

A dramatic change in the educational environment—the shift from grade school to high school which virtually coincides with the onset of puberty—places new demands on the adolescent. Education suddenly becomes a more serious business, the preparation for life work. Choices are often made at the beginning of high school which may have far-reaching implications for the future, for vocation and adult life.

This new high school environment throws the young adolescent into contact with older adolescents who are dating and engaging in other heterosexual activities. To many freshmen the high school junior represents an imposing degree of sophistication and smooth competence in the handling of libidinal urges which to the freshman are new and anxiety-laden. He cannot conceive that he will acquire such competence in the brief space of two additional years. To other young adolescents, the freedom of the high school environment seems to give sanction for acting upon impulses before there has been time to develop mastery and control.

In the home environment too, there are now new parental expectations and attitudes. The re-emergence of early childhood problems and childish behavior creates anxiety in parents that adds to the adolescent crisis. To the bewilderment of their parents, adolescents who were formerly well-adjusted children get involved in difficulties at home, at school, or elsewhere in their environment. Even the fortunate adolescent with loving parents, good character structure and good ego strength rarely escapes completely some upheaval during the difficult adolescent years. It is not surprising if the adolescent, already handicapped by an unstable home, the absence of a parent or crushing economic pressures, shows more serious reactions.

The familiar adolescent rebelliousness incites parents to "lay down the law." They may increase disciplinary measures because they feel this is their last chance to correct defects in their children's behavior and to undo whatever failures in child rearing might previously have occurred. They now fear the adolescent's capacity for serious delinquent behavior.

Parental attitudes change because the parents can no longer view the adolescent as a non-sexual child. Even parents who encouraged early dating and thought it amusing for eleven and twelve-year-olds to attend dances, now worry about the sexual component of dating activities. Intuitively parents see pre-puberty heterosexual relationships as a means of achieving social ease, with tacit recognition that the activity has no real sexual meaning. Puberty forces recognition that the adolescent is capable of engaging in adult sexual behavior.

The ways in which parents react to this recognition vary with the personality and the personal problems of the parents but some change in attitude will inevitably occur. Parents may be suspicious of the adolescent's behavior. By their own feelings they may unconsciously stimulate sexual acting out or convey a sense of guilt about the existence of sexual longings. Parents worry if adolescents delay dating and worry about what occurs when their sons and daughters date. Parents of popular daughters, apprehensive about developing sexuality, try to subdue their dress, make-up and behavior; parents of tomboyish daughters plot to interest the girls in clothing and cosmetics. Shy boys and girls are pushed toward social participation; outgoing ones are urged to stay at home and study. Some parents want to avoid recognition of the adolescent's sexuality and try to continue to think of the adolescent as a non-sexual child. But, since this is unrealistic, it cannot achieve success and the adolescent senses the inappropriateness of the parental attitude.

These varying parental reactions add to the adolescent's confusion. The habitual methods children use to facilitate getting along with their parents and other adults are now shaken, and new methods have to be learned.

The adolescent in turn, cannot accept his parents in the same way he did as a child. His interests are not confined to his immediate family. Home is no longer the safe secure center of life. He does not want to communicate to or share with his parents his total life experiences. Activities and relationships outside the home become more important to the adolescent than his home, which he now begins to use mainly as a base from which to go to his "real life" outside. This change is a drastic one for parents to accept. The child who was an integral and important part of family life becomes a stranger in many ways. Even the adolescent who is so fearful of his sexual impulses that he keeps his outside relationships and activities to a minimum rarely communicates with his family. Parents of an adolescent commonly complain that they no longer understand their child, that he never tells them anything. The opinions of everyone else seem more important to the adolescent than those of his parents. Many parents cannot abdicate gracefully. Their reaction to the changed role creates tension that results in family struggles.

Along with this change in family relationships comes a change in the adolescent's relationship to his peers. Peer group influence is great and the values of the peer group become his important values. These influences may press the adolescent to engage in activities which he himself fears, or is reluctant to do, or would not dare to do alone. But because the group is so significant to him, the adolescent feels impelled to engage in whatever activities are thought important by his particular group which may vary in size from a large delinquent gang to one bosom friend.

The adult world intrudes upon the adolescent. He perceives the structure, the values and the demands of the adult world, the inequities and inconsistencies of society, and this recognition alters his behavior from that of the young child. Adolescents today face a world highly troubled, highly charged and swiftly changing. The accelerated rate of change and the complexities of modern society have enormous impact on the developing adolescent who acts on and is acted upon by the civilization around him.

With characteristic intensity and idealism, the adolescent wants a better world. Whatever the status of his parents, what satisfies them does not satisfy him. When he himself has been victimized because of his race, color or creed he is angry in his demands for equal opportunities. The adolescent does not want to lose his individuality in an automated industrial society. He is impatient with anything that impedes his search for self-fulfillment. As long as he can find activities and interests directed toward fulfillment, his life seems meaningful. If his attempts are unsatisfying, then, while he still retains hope, he tries other, more desperate and perhaps bizarre ways to attain gratification. When hope is gone what follows is despair, depression and alienation. A striking characteristic of all adolescents is that the drive to find fulfillment is expressed in action and deed, rather than in feeling or thought.

Thus, intrapsychic, physical and environmental pressures combine to create the turbulence of adolescence. The change in parental attitudes, conscious or unconscious, the variation in the adolescent's own attitude toward his parents and toward his home, the shift to high school, his perception of the problems of the world, the vastly new importance of his friends act and react upon each other and combine to create a drastically different environment for the adolescent in a relatively short period of time. If, in addition, an adolescent is faced with the reality problems of illness or economic or psychological problems of his parents, of prejudice and discrimination, the stresses may become intolerable.

The special adolescent characteristics call for special treatment techniques. The process of treatment is never easy because human beings are complicated. But those individuals who find that they can live in relative harmony with others, who are comfortable with themselves and the world around them, do not seek treatment. People come for help when they encounter problems they cannot solve alone. The adolescent developmental process itself creates difficulties and counselors encounter the most disturbed of this troubled group.

Adolescents, for the most part, do not come voluntarily for treatment but are referred, usually by those adults involved in their most persistent difficulties. Schools press for treatment for the adolescent with school and/or learning problems, parents call for help with the adolescent who is the focus of difficulty in the family or whose activities create anxieties in them, the courts and the police refer the acting-out adolescent. Pressured to come, apprehensive about what awaits him, the adolescent seldom sees the counselor as a possible source of help.

Yet even with frequent difficulties, the treatment of adolescents can be fruitful. The very factors which bring the adolescent for help, the stresses of adolescence, aid the process. Treatment is made easier by the flexibility of a not yet solidified personality structure. There is hope in adolescents; the world has not yet forced them into resignation. This element of hope offers opportunity for effecting constructive change.

# 2

# Assessment of Adolescent Character Formation

THE MATURATIONAL GOAL of the forces which operate in adolescence is the integration of personality into the consistent definitive groupings of traits which ultimately become the adult character. Character is not finally settled in adolescence but direction takes place during this period toward what will eventually become the mature character.

Character is the total configuration of all the traits, the unique design that distinguishes one individual from another.

Constitutional factors determine body aspects of character but empirical observation as well as genetic studies indicate that character tendencies, perhaps even specific traits of character, may be inherited. Constitutional factors which are the outcome of the intra-uterine development of the foetus and of the effects of birth also contribute to character.

Traumas, physical, emotional or both, which occur during the course of childhood act as magnetic cores around which defenses and adaptations are integrated in ways which become unique to the character of the individual. Deprivation, physical abuse, mentally disturbed parents, parental deaths, illnesses, separations, changes in environment, severe frights, the effects of school, particular teachers or other persons besides the parents as well as many other factors, either as isolated events or as continued forces in the life of every individual, may become determinants in character formation.

In each phase of development specific traits originate which leave their imprint on the total character structure.

From the period of infancy, the oral phase of development, various traits of character, passive and aggressive, are derived which are concerned with basic attitudes about fulfillment of needs in one's self and others. Depending on the nature of this early mother-infant relationship, the groundwork is laid for such personality characteristics as optimism or pessimism, suspiciousness or trustfulness, confidence or insecurity, dependence or independence.

As the child develops locomotion and other motor capacities he becomes able to master his voluntary musculature and to influence his environment. Ability to control anal functions gives the child a sense of personal capacity and mastery, but as he begins to be limited or regulated by his acculturating parents this sense may be enhanced or restricted and evaluated as good or bad. In the process of achieving anal controls the parental standards become clearer and more meaningful and become incorporated into the personality as the conscience or superego. From this, the anal phase of development, the following important characteristics of the personality are derived: sense of mastery, self-evaluation as to acceptability or non-acceptability, feelings of perfection or imperfection, regularity or non-regularity, compulsiveness or non-compulsiveness, praiseworthy or blameworthy, control or lack of control. In addition, because of the strengthening of the musculature, the child can express aggression motorically and from these impulses derive destructive and sadistic traits of character.

In the next phase of development, the oedipal period, the child identifies himself with the parent of the same sex and makes demands for fulfillment on the parent of the opposite sex. Infantile sexual feeling becomes partially localized in the genitalia and the child has sexual fantasies which simulate the parental sexual life. The parent of the same sex becomes a competitive rival for the love of the parent of the opposite sex. Envy and hostility as well as strivings to be superior to the same sex parents are mixed in the child's feelings. These feelings and fantasies are part of the oedipal conflict which is more or less resolved by an identification by the child with the parent of the same sex and a postponement of the insistence on fulfillment of the sexual longings which are then repressed. Personality characteristics which have to do with sexual identity, sexuality in relationships, attitudes toward sexuality and self-evaluations which concern competition in sexual rivalries arise out of this developmental phase and become part of the character organization.

For several years after the oedipal period until pubescence, the child is in a relatively stable phase, the latency period of development. His character structure is grossly organized along familial lines, sexuality is repressed, sublimations become available; he is involved with schooling, he begins to make friends and develop interests outside his home.

The quiescence of the latency period begins to break down prior to the onset of puberty. The child is less complacent, less steady and parental management becomes more difficult. The important hormonal changes of pubescence with the physiological and psychological concomitants shake the total personality. The latency character structure becomes undone and character reintegration and synthesis become the chief developmental tasks of adolescence. While an adolescent already has traits which are unique to him and will remain permanently, there is still fluidity and capacity for modification of personality. This process of character formation continues throughout adolescence before character structure is finally crystallized.

A basic principle of treatment is that diagnosis precedes treatment. Absolute precision diagnostically is, however, impossible because the finest clinical measurements are still very crude when applied to any one particular individual. The difficulty in diagnosis arises from the fact that human beings are complicated and that the differences are frequently quantitative rather than qualitative.

Diagnostic classifications are abbreviated descriptions and no more. Premature or inflexible diagnostic labels may limit treatment disadvantageously. If individuals are fitted into predetermined classifications, the subtler aspects of personality may be missed; human beings cannot be confined within any one phase of personality development. As with fingerprints, the combinations and permutations possible in the development of each individual are innumerable. Each is unique and there are no exact duplications in human personality although there may be in behavior.

The nature of the adolescent personality with its fluidity, its contradictory traits and its variable defensive structure, shifting even during the evaluation process, further complicates diagnostic efforts. The extremes are simple to recognize but most adolescents fall somewhere in between gross pathology and ideal health. Individual practitioners must also guard against the tendency to emphasize what is most apparent to them or what lies within their special focus of interest. To be of maximum use diagnostic assessments should be descriptive of the total dynamic constellation of the individual adolescent. They should relate to the total character traits, to all areas of functioning, internal and environmental, and not merely to transient symptomatic behavior.

It is important at the outset to form broad generalizations about the choice of treatment based on broad diagnostic classifications. This kind of guideline assists in the overall approach, but the initial well-educated guesses should not be confused with more refined and more thorough understanding nor should they substitute for the more completed formulation of the adolescent's functioning. In order to arrive at a more accurate description of the personality than is contained in a diagnostic label, it is necessary to think about each specific piece of behavior and about what is happening in the immediate present in the life of the adolescent. Diagnosis is an evolving process which gains meaning and depth as treatment progresses.

The following important factors need to be considered in the process of assessing the adolescent character formation.

### Management of Impulse

The function of the ego is to manage impulse and to enable the individual to adapt to his environment. In order to appraise character it is less necessary to know about the impulses themselves than to know about the quality of the ego and the superego. The way in which the ego measures out impulses, binds them with rules and regulations, and the ego's management of these rules become an integral part of the character. Ego techniques reveal the characterological development; ego failures reveal the underlying impulses.

Since in each phase of development various impulses dominate, how these were dealt with originally will become part of the characterological composition.

A child whose oral needs early in life were not met adequately will not expect people to gratify him easily. The impulse will be handled either by excessive demands or by the feeling that relationships cannot be counted on for gratification.

Frustrations of motor activity in early infancy may lead to excessive aggression or to passivity. Aggressive impulses start as tension within the individual and the tension is dealt with by muscular activity. When an object is involved the object may be pushed, grabbed, hit, or kicked with the aim of overcoming the tension. When the aggressive activity is prohibited by someone in the environment, the child has to learn to handle the impulse. He may deny or inhibit the impulse so that he is not conscious that he has it; he may decide that it is permissible for him to engage in the activity in spite of the fact that it is evaluated as bad; he may develop guilt over the impulse and become neurotic; he may turn destructive activity into pleasure by a process of erotization with resulting sadism; or, fortunately, he may sublimate the impulse.

Techniques for handling impulses that were used in earlier stages of development may break down in adolescence and new techniques have to be found. These new techniques, discovered in adolescence, ultimately become part of the adult character structure.

## The Nature of the Superego

The superego begins to be formed early in life with the first parental prohibitions, approval for compliance and disapproval for lack of compliance. In the anal developmental phase, the period of achieving mastery, the superego becomes established in the direction that influences its form.

By the time a child reaches latency he has taken over the superego of his parents but without genuine integration and internalization. The unquestioning acceptance of latency is disturbed by the onset of adolescence and the adolescent begins a process of resettling his supergo.

The adolescent is re-forming his standards of morality. In his experimentation he may temporarily abandon hitherto accepted edicts. Even an adolescent with a good superego may be in the process of rebelling against it. In many instances, those adolescents who challenge the community's concepts of proper behavior actually accept the community standards at the same time that they are challenging them out of rebellion, defiance, or a need to test. Adolescents will sometime act out sexually in rebellion against strong superegos.

It is not possible to determine the ultimate quality of the adolescent superego by evaluating any one specific act or incident. The counselor must be sensitive to the total picture and should not form diagnostic conclusions on the basis of any one isolated piece of behavior which is being used as a temporary defensive measure.

Ordinarily, the kind of superego the adolescent will eventually have is similar to that of his parents, regardless of the kind of behavior that is manifest at a given time during adolescence.

The adolescent is also establishing his ego ideal—what he would like to be—a part of his self less punitive in its implications than the superego but related to it. Those individuals who are able to live up to their ego ideals and in accord with their superegos achieve a greater sense of well-being and comfort than those who cannot.

All questions of morality and ethics involve the cultural standards prevalent in the environment. What is acceptable in one culture may be reprehensible in another. Adolescents are quick to say that the standard adult code of ethics is outdated and no longer relevant for their generation. However, basic morality and sexual mores do not change quickly. To be effective the counselor must be secure in his own basic standards, recognize the adolescent need for an ego ideal and yet be aware that ego ideals vary from adolescent to adolescent in subcultures and in differing economic and social strata within the mainstream of the culture. He should keep in mind the ego ideal which appears to be suitable and sensible for any given adolescent and for the culture in which he is living.

Adolescents from subcultural groups often come into conflict with the values of the larger social order. Acceptance of help usually implies a degree of willingness to accept adaptation within at least the broad context of the values of the cultural mainstream. It does not mean an acceptance of the status quo. Within the mainstream there is room for a great deal of variation. No individual needs to deny his own particular cultural heritage or his own social environment in order to benefit from treatment for problems arising from internal pressures or conflicts. Indeed, improved personal integration can lead to more constructive involvement with the social issues of the day.

## MANAGEMENT OF AFFECT

Ordinarily the affective reactions of adolescents are more intense than those of adults. Affects are among the most important human experiences and it is necessary to assess how an adolescent manages affect—whether it is given free rein, whether it is blocked, denied, inhibited or otherwise defended against.

If an adolescent is encouraged to describe in detail the events and occurrences in his life the counselor will learn how he manages affect. He will be sensitive to affective reactions in the adolescent both in the content of an incident and in the manner in which the adolescent recounts it. It is useful to know how the adolescent functions after an event and to note with what affects he describes both the event and his own feelings about it. The counselor should also be aware of the affective responses during the interviews.

Any assessment of character will need to include affective reactions evaluated in terms of appropriateness, control or lack of control.

## INTERPERSONAL RELATIONSHIPS

Observations of relationships and attitudes towards others are also significant aspects of diagnostic assessment. It is important to know how an adolescent is involved with other people and how he thinks about others. The counselor's direct observations of the adolescent in the office in relation to himself give clues to the manner of relating to others.

Relationships are extremely meaningful to adolescents and it is possible to get a good deal of information by asking for examples and descriptions from parents, teachers and from the adolescent himself. Popularity is highly important to high school students. Friendships are greater in adolescence than at any other period in life both in intensity and in number, although they may be transitory. These relationships are usually superficial and their importance tends to lessen in late adolescence and adulthood.

During adolescence the importance exists because of a great need for others, for interaction with them and as a way of proving self worth. Narcissistic sensitivity is great and the young adolescent reacts acutely to relationships. He may feel superior or inferior, accepted or rejected, normal or strange; the differences are an important part of his character. Later, as adolescents become more settled, have more direction and knowledge of themselves, as their goals for life become more certain, the intensity of this need for peer approval diminishes.

### MANAGEMENT OF RESPONSIBILITY AND LIFE ROUTINES

Areas of life function rather than specific symptoms are important in understanding adolescent character. How an adolescent manages his life reveals the specific techniques his ego has acquired and how these contribute to his character formation. It is helpful to know how an adolescent handles the details of his life, how he manages his time, his effectiveness in school or on a job if he has one, his responsibility in relation to household chores and other duties, how he arranges opportunities for activities and relationships.

Some adolescents, particularly those with compulsive characters, will spend a good deal of time giving these details but ordinarily the counselor will need to be alert in order to catch clues which indicate the adolescent's life style in order to evaluate this aspect of his character.

In a sense school is for the adolescent what work is for an adult. But adolescents do not look upon school as an essential part of their lives in the same way that adults regard their occupations. Many adolescents, even those who function well in school, view education as a preparation, a means to an end, rather than as a value in itself. Some adolescents think of school as a means of killing time. For others, school may take on different psychological meanings, oedipal issues of competition, the need to please or to rebel against parents. But most adolescents see school as a requirement and react to it in their characteristic method of handling requirements.

No matter how the adolescent views school, the way he fulfills this responsibility reveals aspects of his character. Defenses will be evident, controls or their lack, sublimations if these are involved. Clues will appear as to the nature of the superego and the ego ideal in his involvement with or indifference to educational values, in his attitudes about doing work independently or copying, and his relationships to his peers and his teachers.

## GOALS AND DIRECTION

A life goal is an ego ideal in the largest sense. It includes the way an individual sees himself in the present and in the future. Everyone has a picture of himself in the stream of life. The adolescent's ego ideal may be unrealistic and the adolescent usually places fulfillment of goals far off into the future; but all adolescents have some kind of ego ideal. One measure of mental health is the quality of this ego ideal and its realistic possibilities for satisfaction in life.

Adolescents may not speak spontaneously about their goals, but the counselor should be able to learn the aims which motivate the adolescent and the means by which he gives direction to fulfilling these goals.

There are some adolescents who develop ego ideals about careers quite early in life, either through an early positive identification with a loved person, or through an activity that fulfills fantasy or a combination of both. The child who plays with blocks may fulfill a fantasy as he builds a tower, and as he grows older may find more complicated building toys from which he gets satisfaction. If this same child has a loving father who is a carpenter, early in his life the child may be motivated toward a career in which building is involved; he may decide to become an architect. He derives primitive satisfaction from the original infantile fantasy which can be socially acceptable and which is available for fulfillment as a vocation. From the identification with his father this career choice also fulfills a sense of identity as a man. Such a choice does not have a neurotic or conflictual basis; it is a mode of satisfaction found early in life out of sublimation of primitive needs and through identification.

Some goals are not sublimations but arise out of a neurotic structure. Other career choices are the result of a combination of conflict resolution and adaptive sublimations. In adolescence these early vocational choices may find their final form or take a direction which ultimately leads to the final choice.

For those career choices which are made early in life to be successful there must be intellectual capacity and basic talent which can find opportunity for expression and can obtain the support and interest of the community. Some choices, as for instance artistic, or innovating scientific aims, may run counter to the wishes of parents or to the contemporary community but where there is great talent or skill, such choices may ultimately find justification.

Some adolescents have conflict in fulfilling ego ideals which are seemingly natural to their families and their environment. The son of a successful business man who likes his father may, in adolescence, develop a disdain for money and declare a preference for working with his hands. Examination of this choice can determine what forces led the boy away from the expected career choice.

When a single specific ego ideal becomes the whole measure of the individual's self-evaluation, he may not have sufficient resilience in his personality to shift to a different vocational goal if reality requires this of him. Such a rigid vocational choice stems from and contributes to a serious limitation in personality development. Often the vocational goal of an adolescent, whatever its source, may be highly disruptive to his personality equilibrium and to the course of his life and such goals then become a problem. If career goals are primarily based on conflict resolution it is likely that there will be frequent episodes of psychic conflict. If the goal is impossible of attainment it is also a problem.

Unfortunately many people do not have the opportunity completely to fulfill their ideal vocational goals but out of necessity, and the realities of their environment, are forced into work which is uncongenial to their personal inclinations.

Examining the kind of career goal an adolescent has helps the counselor know the dynamics of his character structure. Different forces will be responsible for choices based on identification, on early gratification, on conflict resolution or on combinations of these influenced by environmental factors.

## RELATIONSHIP TO THE COMMUNITY

The way an adolescent sees his place in relationship to others, his feelings about his community, and about social, political and religious issues, also affect his ego ideal. These attitudes give a picture of his identity. This aspect of identity, however, is highly variable, is not an integrated part of the self in early adolescence and usually manifests itself only in late adolescence. Community identity is a kind of top layer less deeply ingrained into the character than other aspects of the ego ideal.

There are exceptions however. A person born into a large family may grow up as part of the group and later have positive group or community interests as an adult. Living with and for others becomes an essential part of his ego ideal. The group interest may have a negative basis also. It can be a reaction formation to not having received desired gratification in the large family setting. Group interest and activity may be an effort to perpetuate the competition of the family. There are more subtle variations also.

Some politically inclined adolescents have megalomanic fantasies of greatness which lead to involvement in public life in order to fulfill these unconscious fantasies. This need not be pathological depending on the way the individual functions. Public leadership probably requires narcissism and some elements of primitive megalomania, but as long as the fantasies remain unconscious and are fulfilled in socially acceptable ways, they are not considered pathological.

The adolescent's search for fixed stars, his readiness for ideals, his need for moral and ethical values combine to make him more inclined to religious instruction than earlier and ready to cope with religious issues. Confirmation ceremonies are ego supportive in establishing his identity as an adult member of a church. Graduation from Sunday School is an important step. Participation in affairs of the church may be an important means to counteract the effects of his membership in typically adolescent groups of dubious or no ethical values.

Young adolescents may not yet be interested in community values. The high degree of narcissism precludes serious concern about the community. But from school and other activities the counselor gets clues as to the trend of his community interest and potential involvement. Older adolescents, in the college years, are often in the forefront of important social and political issues of the day. These activities are undertaken with a dedication and intensity that adults are rarely capable of investing. The adolescent convictions about principles tend to be more firmly held than those of adults. These "idealistic" activities should be evaluated on their own merits by those who are concerned with the issues. The fact that adolescent dynamics are involved does not invalidate the activity nor determine the validity of the issue itself.

The counselor however must understand that the ego ideal of the adolescent is being forged in these interests and activities and some important values which may or may not accrue to this identity will be found in them. The counselor will need to determine whether or not the specific activity contributes to personality deviation, or to the enrichment and enlargement of the adolescent's identity.

## CHARACTER ORIENTATION TOWARDS PSYCHOLOGICAL LIFE

A well integrated individual is in touch with what goes on inside himself without being immobilized by introspection. Without any introspection personality tends to be shallow. A counselor will want to know, or be able to form, a good estimate of the adolescent's capacity for introspection. The introspective adolescent can come to understand how he functions. Adolescents who have never before been directed to pay attention to inner life can often be helped to become introspective. When an adolescent is oriented only to outer reality and never thinks about his psychological life, he is using a high degree of defensiveness against inner perception. This may be indicative of serious disturbance. On the other hand there are many individuals who are not introspective in their character formations because such perception has not been part of their personality development.

## IDENTITY

The establishment of a firm sense of identity is one of the major tasks of adolescence. Most of the character structure is involved in the identity. No appraisal of the character formation of the adolescent can be complete without evaluation of how far he has progressed in knowing who he is and what he thinks about himself. (See chapter on Identity.)

In summary, examining, thinking about and describing the foregoing areas and affects of functioning help in understanding character formation. A description of the adolescent character formation will emerge from consideration of these criteria. Then, if necessary, a diagnostic name may be chosen and attached. It is not the category but the understanding that is important. Counselors deal with what the adolescent brings and the treatment follows understanding of the functioning personality.

## CHARACTER DISORDER

A character disorder is a condition in which the character integration is a maladaptive one; the personality is crystallized in a manner which interferes with adequate functioning in life.

Since the capacity for adaptation to varying circumstances and to the standard expectations of the environment are measures of mental health, the principles of flexibility and cultural adaptation are the externally observable reference points for determining deviation from adequate functioning. As the diagnostic process evolves, it is also important to determine the internal psychic content and its influence on the behavior and well-being of the individual.

Because adolescent characters are still in the process of formation, the term character disorder should be used cautiously. The emphasis in character appraisal should rather be on whatever pathology exists within the developing personality structure. Adolescent character integration is an on-going process and the terms character trends or direction of character formation more accurately convey the sense of the as yet unfinished process. Crystallized character structure in a malfunctioning adolescent indicates serious pathological disorder. This early solidification is not usually seen but only when it has occurred should an adolescent be diagnosed as having a character disorder.

## Differentiating the Psychotic from the Non-Psychotic

Traditionally diagnosis is divided into separate entities such as the psychoses, the neuroses, the character disorders and the organic disorders. The last is a truly separate entity. The others, however, bear many similarities. Psychosis does not differ from neurosis in an absolute sense but mainly by a quantitative difference, especially in the ego. All psychotics suffer from inner problems as well as problems of external reality, and all neurotics have some difficulty in the external world, struggles in interpersonal relationships, as well as inner conflicts. Sometimes the differentiation is made that the ego of the psychotic distorts reality while the ego of the neurotic does not. But this is not always true. Under stress and the pressure of internal conflicts neurotics may also distort reality.

Adolescence has been called "normal psychosis" and indeed there are many adolescent mental functions which are similar to those of psychotics. But most normal and neurotic adolescents go to school, study, relate to their peers, get along reasonably well with their parents and teachers, enjoy many pleasures and are in good contact with reality whatever the adolescent peculiarities; their total functioning is not psychotic.

Any counselor who deals with adolescents should be able to distinguish between psychotic and non-psychotic adolescent manifestations. Familiarity with the mechanisms that are common to adolescents and with those that are explicitly psychotic will aid in this differentiation, will make for better understanding of the non-psychotic adolescent and will enable the counselor to deal with those psychotic adolescents who can benefit from non-institutional treatment.

Psychotic adolescents use a great many defenses including many of the neurotic defenses that are common in adolescence. One broad generalization, however, is that the use of very primitive ego mechanisms characterizes psychotics. Also, in the main, psychotic defenses are primarily directed at altering or dealing with external realities while neurotic defenses are primarily directed against the internal fantasy life.

Normal or neurotic behavior may best be differentiated from psychotic by the evaluation of the total adaptation. Problems indicative of psychosis include: extreme withdrawal from social participation; extreme passivity or submission to discipline; over-conventional behavior with the inability to deviate from fixed standards in any way; repeated hallucinations; fixed delusions; repeated violent eruptions; bizarre fantasies and the lack of capacity for empathy.

It is difficult for psychotics to involve themselves in the external world. Either they resist all changes or they are susceptible to every changing whim with inability to follow through on anything. There is also frequently a loss of the capacity to control or postpone action.

Many of the phenomena observed in non-psychotic adolescents are suggestive of psychotic pathology. Isolated symptoms are not in themselves proof of psychosis and must be evaluated in the context of the total personality. Adolescents may use psychotic defenses transiently without being psychotic.

Most psychoses do not appear suddenly without warning. Where there is serious psychopathology the past history will usually indicate a personality with a serious defect. It is essential that the counselor secure as much information as it is possible from all sources about the adolescent's total functioning. It is important to understand the presence and the nature of any special stresses the adolescent may be undergoing and reacting to at the given time. The counselor should recognize the possibility that any incident or piece of behavior, no matter how bizarre, may be transitory in nature. The ego capacity to maintain good integration and the ego ability to reintegrate and function adequately soon after any isolated psychotic appearing incident must be evaluated.

The counselor who has been working with a variety of adolescents over a period of time will develop an ability to sense integration even in what may seem like disintegration. He will be able to feel the difference between psychosis and nonpsychosis from the subtle psychic aura even before he can formulate the factors on which the differentiation is based. When there is any element of doubt the counselor should arrange for psychiatric consultation and or examination. Usually psychotic adolescents are too disturbed to remain at large in the community and for their own protection require hospitalization and specialized treatment.

# 3

# The Adolescent Ego

AN INDIVIDUAL COMES to adolescence with an ego that has developed out of his specific predispositions, constitutional as well as psychological, and out of his total life experience. By the time of adolescence the ego has already acquired a characteristic structure and characteristic techniques of adaptation that were suitable to the maintenance of some kind of equilibrium. With puberty the quantity of instinctual energy sharply increases. The sudden intensification of both sexual and aggressive impulses creates a new experience in quality and in quantity.

The great turmoil of adolescence is a result of the intensity of instinctual demands on an ego unprepared to meet them. Sexual and aggressive demands existed prior to adolescence. By the end of the oedipal period, any impulses that will ever exist are present. Any change that takes place subsequently is quantitative, a change in intensity. Individual variations occur in the strength of specific impulses at all developmental levels, but the impulses are not new. Aggressive impulses are always present, even in utero. Little boys and girls have some pleasant genital sensations. There may be longing for relationships of a sexual nature in the latency period. But the intensity of adolescent instinctual demands is missing from the earlier sensations and it is this intensity which confronts the adolescent ego.

Infantile impulses are revived in adolescence. Although they have been modified by subsequent developmental experience they now strongly insist on gratifications which are not readily available and not wholly acceptable to the adolescent. The oedipal conflict, quiescent during latency, is reawakened and must be resolved. At the same time there is a strong maturational pull in the direction of adult independence and self-determination. The childhood ego mechanisms are inadequate to keep the intensified impulses in check and of little value in discharging tension. It is as if the adolescent were an immigrant adjusting to a new way of life in an unfamiliar land. Parents sense this when they complain, as they frequently do, that their adolescent children have become strangers.

Some have described the adolescent ego, shaken under attack, as a weak ego. The person with a weak ego has an insufficient amount of energy to maintain his defenses, either because of congenital insufficiency of energy, or because of stresses which have depleted the ego so that it does not have the adaptive or defensive strength that it once had, or might have had in different circumstances.

When the adequacy or strength of the ego is evaluated, the amount of stress the ego has had to face must be considered. The same ego will react differently to different amounts of stress, either internal or external.

Also the ego should be evaluated in terms of the energy available for functioning. Sometimes an ego is labeled weak when what is meant is a poor ego. A person who gets enraged over minor frustrations may not have a weak ego. He may have a great deal of energy available, but the energy is not being used in an adaptive manner. It is being discharged in aggressive action and not employed in restraint of the aggressive impulses. Insufficient energy is directed into repressing or controlling rage, even though the ego is strong and there is a great deal of available energy. Some people with considerable energy in the ego still have poor egos. For example, paranoid schizophrenics or compulsive characters both have a great deal of energy but poor egos. The quantity of energy available determines whether an ego is weak or strong. The quality of defense or adaptation determines whether an ego is poor or good. Most weak egos are poor, but not all strong egos are good.

An adolescent needs a strong ego to withstand the barrage of intensified impulse. The problem most frequently is not the weakness of the adolescent ego but maladaptive ego control of strong impulses. The kind of apathy that indicates an inadequate ego is rarely seen except in the severely ill adolescent. Until he has discovered adequate ego techniques for resisting the expression of impulse, the adolescent may give in to impulse simply because the strength of the drives is greater than the ability to control. The adolescent who acts out sexually or engages in delinquent behavior and then says, "I could not help it," is stating this psychological fact.

Acting out is ordinarily considered undesirable, yet in a sense acting out of impulses is the very process of living; if everything were left at the level of fantasy or thought, nothing would ever get accomplished in the world. It is important to evaluate the form of acting out. People act on impulse or unconscious fantasies but also on conscious thought. Conscious action cannot ever be completely separated from unconscious processes; both are always present. But the quality of action changes at different periods of life.

Adolescents act on impulse or on fantasy; the adolescent superego is not an adult superego. Adolescents have not yet fully absorbed the values of the adult world. Society expects and accepts some forms of action from an adolescent which would be considered inappropriate for a grownup.

An adult may not wish to get out of bed to go to work but his sense of responsibility pushes him to do so. The dictates of a mature integrated superego affect ego action; the way an individual functions determines his maturity. An adolescent might stay in bed in spite of his conscious knowledge that he has a responsibility to go to school. He can yield to his impulse to stay in bed with less conscious and unconscious distress than an adult who takes the same action. The parallel actions of an adolescent who misses school and an adult who fails to go to work arise out of different psychological bases.

Activity is characteristic of adolescence. A fourteen-year-old boy, even one whose problems center around too rigid controls, may, as he talks with his counselor, actually demonstrate the exercises he performs to develop his biceps. An adult would limit himself to talking about this activity. But it is quite appropriate for an adolescent to demonstrate directly by physical action.

Along with the physiological changes of puberty, the great and sudden increase in psychic energy intensifies not only the instinctual impulses but the ego functions as well. The stubbornness, determination, and willfulness of adolescents emanate from intensified ego activity. It accounts, too, for the dedication and devotions seen in the adolescent, the passion of his love affairs and the intensity he experiences in his sublimated activities.

Because of this great amount of available energy the adolescent ego is able to face and master the stressful tasks of this developmental period and reach maturity, usually with adequate integration.

This energy is available to all the ego functions; it may be directed to undesirable as well as desirable forms of adaptation. When character disorders appear in adolescents, they can be modified only with the greatest difficulty because the pathological integration is maintained with great intensity. Tremendous energy is invested in the defenses which are often impenetrable. The adolescent delinquent may be as dedicated to his delinquency as the adolescent artist to his art.

The adolescent may invest his great fund of energy in success or in failure. He operates as if his days held more than twenty-four hours. When the push is toward successful use of energy, he can maintain a good academic record, hold a part-time job and have a full recreational life. When his investment is in failure, he uses an equal amount of energy. When he has decided to act, and the decision may be premature or based on misconceptions or misinformation, he will do so in spite of warnings, advice, or his own knowledge that his behavior is detrimental to himself. This great investment in the decision is the ego's proud effort to maintain the validity of its own actions without interference from an adult. In such instances the adolescent is in effect saying, "This may be wrong, but at least it is my own decision." The normal adolescent ultimately will evaluate properly the effect of his decisions and modify his behavior. The right to self-determination is the assumed prerogative of the adolescent.

Pathology is determined, not by the willfulness that is almost universal in adolescents, but by the nature of the action taken. It is also determined by the persistence of poor judgment in the face of corrective measures and recognized harmful consequences. Counselors may sense that some youngsters are stubbornly insistent on their own destruction. This characteristic is frequently found among adolescent acting-out delinquents.

Faced with the monumental task of integrating all the new stresses, the adolescent ego flounders. The awkward stumbling results from trying out many kinds of mechanisms in the effort to maintain equilibrium. The chief characteristic of the adolescent ego is the variable and unpredictable nature of the defenses it uses. The typical fluctuations and alterations are the attempt to find workable adaptations. But whatever the difficulties past or present, the ego has within it, as a basic function, the adaptive tendency, the drive toward mastery. Normally the floundering is neither intense nor persistent before the adolescent ego begins to find solutions.

The adolescent can use only those techniques that are within his own repertoire of defenses and adaptations. He therefore begins the adaptive process by selecting from that repertoire those defenses that worked earlier because they seem most likely to help with the new pressures. He does not go through a chrono-logical sequence to search for workable adaptations; it is not an orderly process. The adolescent moves backward and forward, sampling his store of formerly serviceable defenses and adapta-tions, discarding some, trying others over and over, and forming new ones as the old fail to serve their purpose. This seemingly random use of the techniques that served him when he was pre-pubescent accounts for the bizarre qualities seen in some adolescents which may, at times, be mistaken for a psychotic process. It accounts for the frequent complaints of parents about the behavior of their adolescent children. Parents find it hard to understand a fifteen-year-old who whines like a baby one moment and argues like a trial lawyer the next.

Regression, progression and synthesis are continued processes throughout the adolescent development. The alternations, com-binations and fusions of defenses and adaptations depend on the earlier personality structure, on the day-to-day stresses and on the external and internal forces which press the adolescent ego to the election of one or another mechanism of adjustment. The adolescent ego is flexible, experimental and versatile. These characteristics account for the unstructured nature of the per-sonality as compared with the latency child or with the adult.

Because the adolescent is a "freshman" his ego is inexperi-enced in dealing with the numerous difficult tasks which con-front it. The trial-and-error nature of its experimentation makes the ego appear fluctuating, unsettled and inconsistent. These characteristics, together with the tendency to use regressive in-fantile defenses create the impression that the adolescent ego is weak, fragile and vulnerable. It has even prompted the com-parison of normal adolescents to psychotics, but the similarities are deceptive, not real. These very characteristics are the strength of the adolescent; they are his stock in trade.

Understanding the normal characteristics of the adolescent ego is essential if there is to be successful differentiation between the pathological and non-pathological. The task is complicated because the very nature of the adolescent development makes possible a wide variety of ego mechanisms within the limits of normality. The counselor who works with adolescents must be able to evaluate properly the educability, the resiliency and the versatility of an ego that can afford to experiment with many varieties of adaptive techniques, must sense the inner firmness, the integrity and the constancy of personality which exist in spite of the intensity of the impulses, the apparent regressive defenses, and the myriad changes of this developmental period.

Flexibility and versatility of defense are part of the normal maturational process. These ego characteristics make the adolescent amenable and responsive to influential relationship and permit reorganization of the personality. Because there is a multitude, almost a conglomeration, of defenses from all levels of development there is opportunity to select and to establish those that will be most useful. The unusual amount of energy available to the adolescent ego is manifested in resiliency, resourcefulness, determination and great potential strength—strength to handle the pressing impulses and the ever-present conflicts. A strong ego can be shaken in the process, but it takes a strong ego to achieve the adolescent developmental goals and the integration of a mature personality.

# 4

# Adaptive Regressions
# in Adolescence

THE ADOLESCENT EGO experiments because it must accomplish
many unfamiliar tasks. Among the attempts at adaptation are
regressions, the repetition of earlier patterns of mastery. Regression is usually considered pathological but it can also be an
adaptive mechanism. Sleep, for example, is a universal temporary regression, necessary and beneficial. Adolescent regressions
may go back to any previous developmental level. Even deep regressions to primitive functions, ordinarily psychotic if observed
in adults, may still be within the limits of normality for adolescents. The regressive adaptations are most evident early in
adolescence but they continue throughout the adolescent period
with varying frequency, duration and intensity.

These infantile forms of behavior in adolescents are displayed as impatience, demandingness, chronic hunger and in-
satiability, dissatisfaction and irritability. Heightened narcissism
in adolescents is evident in increased self-consciousness, concerns with the body, dreams of glory, excessive pride and poignant sensitivity. Destructiveness, disorderliness, recalcitrance and
slovenliness are indications of anal revolt against the expectations and restrictions imposed upon the adolescent.

Adolescent regression is similar to the retreat of an army. Military retreat permits redeployment and reorganization of troops, the addition of reinforcements, and planning for new defensive and offensive maneuvers. In like manner adolescent regressions allow opportunity for the conservation and redistribution of energy, the reevaluation of current techniques for handling anxieties, the resolution of problems past and present, and the planning of subsequent ego maneuvers.

Regressive behavior reduces the pressures stemming from the expectations of parents or other people for premature adult behavior. Generally parents expect an adolescent to act more like a grownup than a small child, but when they observe infantile behavior in the adolescent they are forced to recognize their expectations are premature. In effect, then, the regressions provide breathing space for the adolescent, buy additional time before assuming adult behavior.

Unacceptable emotions can be expressed with greater impunity when the adolescent is childish. The adolescent who says, "I hate you" to his parents in an infantile manner does not get the same angry response as he would if his statement were adult in tone and quality.

As he re-experiences previously unacceptable infantile forms of behavior the adolescent finds that this kind of behavior is incompatible with his ego ideal which is modeled after an adult pattern. His experimentation results in modification of the infantile behavior. This process is reinforced both by the parents and by the environment.

Some of the more useful childhood adaptations are revived and modified; they lose their childlike qualities, are reintegrated or fused into the new adolescent character. Other personality characteristics are discarded as no longer acceptable or valuable. Many sublimations come into being during this regressive experimental phase that continue successfully into adult life.

As temporary or periodic measures regressions permit alleviation of stress, lessening of tension, building up of energy; they may implement creativity through fantasy. Were the regressions to be persistent they might be considered as possible signs of pathology. Further, if the regressions take place within the context of a personality or of behavior which includes chronic school difficulty, neglect of other responsibilities, social isolation and inattention, they might be considered evidence of pre-schizophrenic disorder. The significance depends on the place of any particular piece of behavior in the total personality.

Extreme libidinal regressions are often observed in adolescents but ego regressions, although they may occur, are ordinarily not as enduring nor as extreme. The ego regresses chiefly in the sense that the adolescent ego may act on impulse. The nature of the action, however, is not often truly infantile but is determined by reality considerations of the particular adolescent's life. Some forms of ego regression are tolerantly accepted by society even in adults. Members of fraternal organizations wear comical hats and indulge in infantile pranks at a convention although these same adults would not tolerate similar behavior in themselves or others when the convention has adjourned.

Although the regressions which occur to some extent in all adolescents are disturbing and sometimes appear strange and deviant, they are not in themselves pathological. On the contrary they are an integral part of the developmental process of adolescence.

The adolescent regressions have the following distinct qualities which differentiate them from the regressions in true pathological states.

They are temporary and transitional rather than chronic and fixed.

They are not totally acceptable to the adolescent ego ideal and the ego reacts to them with varying degrees of anxiety, shame and guilt.

No actual breakdown occurs in the sense of reality perception or in the thought processes. The adolescent fantasies may be extravagant or may verge on the bizarre but when the adolescent is confronted with his fantasy, he acknowledges it as fantasy and makes explanations and rationalizations that are logical, comprehensible and meaningful, although not always acceptable.

The regressions are altered or modified by important relationships. The unkemptness of the girl-hater at thirteen yields to the fastidiousness of the adolescent of sixteen absorbed in his first love affair. The adolescent suffering from pathology may remain slovenly and unaffected by any heterosexual relationship.

Many adolescent regressions are substantially influenced in nature by peer associations and frequently appear in all the members of a group. The form of the regression may also be group or culturally determined rather than emerging solely out of the unique intra-psychic state of the individual as in the pathologies. The fainting and screaming at rock-and-roll performances is diagnostically differentiated from an individual hysterical reaction; the members of the college panty-raid horde do not suffer from the same disorders as the sexually deviant or schizoid thief of women's undergarments.

Careful study of the present life situation and behavior of the adolescent reveals that the regressive behavior produces maladaptation only to a limited extent or in an isolated area of the adolescent's life. The behavior may be cause for complaint by the parents or by the school, but usually not both; it may be a complaint expressed by the adolescent himself. It is not all-pervasive and persistent in producing maladjustment as in the more serious clinical disorders.

Examination of the history of the adolescent shows that the regressive behavior under scrutiny is not consistent with the total developmental pattern. It seems isolated from the rest of the picture both in the past and in the present life situation. In most instances of pathology, the preadolescent personality already showed signs of, and the dynamics for, the pathological ego mechanisms. Moreover in the pathologies there are many other indications of disturbance and the regression is not an isolated characteristic. For the normal adolescent, the general orientation of the personality is towards normal adjustment.

The unconscious implications of adolescent regressions remain unconscious. For example, if a normal adolescent boy is asked why he overeats he will give a simple answer such as that he is growing or that he is hungry. A seriously disturbed adolescent, on the other hand, may say that eating is the only pleasure he has in life, or that unless he keeps eating he will die.

The adolescent regressions are purposeful, almost as if the ego chooses to try the device to determine if it will resolve the pressing problems at hand. There is actually some degree of conscious ego control although primarily it is an unconscious process. Sensing this quality of electiveness is extremely important in differentiating the normal from the pathological. In the pathological ego the regression is beyond the ego's control; with the normal adolescent the behavior is a device of the ego.

In the seriously disturbed or pathological adolescent, the regressive behavior is part of a loosely knit structure, and lapses can be felt in the emotional affect and the meaning of the communication that takes place in treatment. With the regressed adolescent the counselor is aware, in the intimacy of the interpersonal relationship, of interaction with an integrated, comprehensible personality.

## SELECTED ADAPTIVE REGRESSIONS

### Perceptual

Creative writers can sometimes recapture, and some adolescents can describe the heightened perceptions of adolescence, an exaggerated awareness of physical sensations which has probably not existed since early infancy.

In modified form the adolescent allows himself to indulge in perceptions the way an infant does. The infant ego is predominantly aware of itself and is unable to distinguish the self from the non-self. At that period of life the ego is exquisitely and exclusively preoccupied with its own functioning, hearing, seeing, feeling, touching. The infant is bombarded with stimuli which have no meaning because there is no past experience around which to organize reactions to the stimuli. The ego responds simply by perceiving the stimuli in a confused and unregulated manner. The infant is acutely aware of bodily sensations, of stimuli from within and without, but is unable to put them together, or to separate them.

A similar process occurs in early adolescence. The adolescent ego can regress to such primitive narcissistic phases of functioning and still continue the ego functions of recent acquirement. Adolescents often describe their sensations of the shifting boundaries of the world around them. They may speak of feeling lost, or smothered. They may even be aware of the surge of primitive feelings and perceptive disorientations in time or place.

Quite commonly adolescents have sensations of unorganized bodily processes. They have peculiar pains, they think they have serious diseases and they may become almost hypochondriacal. Adolescents sometimes feel strange to themselves, indicating that they do not accurately perceive their own body image.

Normal adults may have transitory primitive ego feelings or affect states in which they are overwhelmed by the perception of color or sound. Without losing the sense of reality, and keeping the sensation within bounds, people can get caught up in perception, as, for example, in listening to music. Unconscious memories are evoked; the ego is flooded by personal associations. The normal ego can allow sensations to sweep over it and can indulge temporarily in primitive fantasy without becoming engulfed. Some disassociation of this kind is even necessary for esthetic enjoyment; there is less pleasure in strict objectivity and intellectualization. The sensitive or creative person responds to the arts not only with his conscious knowledge but also with unconsciously determined feelings. In weak egos, persistence of these perceptive states creates serious pathology because the sensations interfere with reality testing. Such egos become overwhelmed by their own perceptions and are not able to differentiate the personally toned experience from reality.

Adolescents have many perceptive experiences that parallel adult esthetic response. The exquisite sensitivity to perceptive experience is a recrudescence of an infantile ego function but this does not depreciate the value of this experience, unless it interferes with the total functioning of the adolescent. The significance of any single function cannot be determined in isolation from the remainder of the personality functioning.

Some adolescents read much meaning into the unique quality of their perceptions and are able to make rich experiences of them. Inarticulate adolescents cannot describe these sensations except perhaps by calling them strange or funny, but they, too, have them. Sometimes these perceptions are so absorbing that they interfere with the adolescent's functioning, often they are transient and do not create problems for the adolescent. Some adolescents defend against too vivid perceptions in order to function more successfully in their world. They quickly stop introspecting and turn themselves to the external world which is better structured than their chaotic inner sensations. This acute adolescent sensitivity is usually lost later in life. In some individuals, however, these ego states are articulated and may persist to a greater or lesser degree as they grow up to become sensitive and creative adults.

The vividness of adolescent perceptions is so compelling that some people—adolescents or adults with adolescent personalities —try to create it for themselves. At one time or another opium, cocaine, alcohol, marijuana and more recently, LSD have been used to attain heightened experiences. Some individuals experiment while alone but others find the permission to "let go" in a group or at a party, although they might not dare the attempt alone. Most efforts at consciousness expansion result in heightened affect and emotional experience without improved intellectual function or creativity. Unfortunately, in too many instances, these drugs have led to deteriorated states, psychosis, and even suicide.

*Narcissistic*

Narcissus, in the Greek legend, is a youth, an adolescent. His is an adolescent regression; the image he sees in the water and with which he falls in love is a reflection of his own self. The self is the object of the ego's love to the young adolescent. He is in love with himself, with his mental functioning and with all of his capacities.

Narcissism may be used defensively at any period in life to compensate for feelings of inferiority but some degree of narcissistic regression is common in adolescence.

## 1. Love of Self

The adolescent feels that the world revolves around him. He is deeply, almost desperately, concerned with himself. Adolescents are self-centered and self-conscious in a quite literal sense. Unconsciously everyone longs to be the center of the world but the adolescent feels this as a conscious or preconscious state. Older people sometimes envy this capacity in adolescents; later in life experiences are not so vivid or so rich and some adults look back upon their adolescence with nostalgia. The preoccupations with the self, the experiences and the feelings that accompany this extreme self-involvement are frequently remembered with longing as pleasurable.

## 2. Preoccupation with the Body

The adolescent is aware of the growth of his body, of the physical changes that are occurring. This concern with the body is not entirely in relation to appearance although partly it is the desire to be attractive. Ultimately this body preoccupation is valuable for the establishment of heterosexual relationships but there is also in early adolescence considerable narcissistic investment in concern with the body that is directed towards the establishment of the sense of self. Long periods of staring in the mirror, so typical of adolescents, are reminiscent of the infant's absorbed study of his hands and feet. The adolescent studies himself to take in the wonder and the strangeness of the loved object—himself.

## 3. Megalomanic

Adolescents are absorbed in their own ideas, thoughts and feelings. Often they overevaluate their own mental capacities. They see themselves as discovering new ideas and new attitudes and this is one of the reasons why they almost always feel that their parents are old-fashioned and out-of-date. Intellectual or articulate adolescents express their feelings about their abilities and discuss the megalomanic process going on in themselves sometimes with little shame or embarrassment. Even a nonverbal, nonintellectual adolescent may be convinced that he has unique capacities. Adolescents fairly commonly believe that they could win a fortune gambling, or make a million in the stock market, with no risk of loss, because of their own special powers.

Often adolescents come upon an idea which they think is a brilliant new discovery of their own. When subsequently they learn that others have already formulated the same thought they are then not apt to think that they are heirs of the world's accumulated knowledge but rather that they could have originated great concepts equal to those of the geniuses of the past if they had been fortunate enough to have been born earlier.

Adolescents tend toward megalomanic expectations, tend to exaggerate the possibilities for fulfillment and achievement because their egos have not yet had sufficient experience in the frequently harsh realities of living to recognize that all desires cannot be gratified. The strong impulses of adolescents increase the tendency to unrealistic megalomania; by its very nature megalomania is an expectation of the hope for the fulfillment of the impulses on a grandiose scale. Megalomania represents a basic demand for complete gratification.

Extreme megalomania in an adolescent is indicative of either of two different ego states. The first is a defect of the ego which permits the adolescent to be more than normally unrealistic. Inability to accept the realities of existence leads him to accept the idea that every wish of his will be ultimately fulfilled.

The second type of adolescent megalomanic defense represents an attempt to overcome feelings of inferiority, inadequacy and dissatisfaction. Feeling inadequate, the adolescent defends by overcompensating. He allows himself to fantasy that he can fulfill any impulse, although underneath he senses that he really cannot. From this mechanism may stem the frequent adolescent fantasy of becoming famous without effort. In the healthy adolescent, constructive elements can be observed in his efforts to fulfill his fantasy. It is normal for adolescents to be ambitious, to have fantasies of great achievement and great expectations for the future.

The megalomanic defense will be affected differently by some actual success in achievement depending on whether or not the adolescent ego is good. In the adolescent with an adequate ego, the megalomania will be gratified by the nature of his actual achievement. It may become a sublimation, that is, the adolescent will direct himself to achieve in order to fulfill the unconscious megalomanic fantasy, within the confines of reality. In the more pathological adolescent whose ego is not well structured, some degree of successful achievement may aggrandize his megalomanic fantasy and the fantasy may not be accompanied by constructive ego effort. This is because the more pathological adolescent does not have the ego capacity to realize that successful achievement may result from many factors or combinations of factors such as some special opportunity, or luck, as well as hard work. His ego remains under the illusion that his success is due entirely to his own rare talents and any small degree of successful achievement is reinforcement of his false notions. The megalomanic fantasies therefore are not modified, magical thinking and other devices come into play, deepening the idea that wishes can be fulfilled without serious effort.

If an adolescent has succeeded in some kind of achievement but his parents are hard to please and react by asking why the adolescent did not do still better, the adolescent may respond in various ways. He may become depressed, with the feeling that nothing he can do will satisfy his parents; he may give up further efforts with a "what's the use?" or he may become more megalomanic in his fantasy life, dreaming of an achievement stupendous enough to impress his parents.

When parents are themselves megalomanic, or live vicariously through the over-evaluated achievements of their child, elaborating the fantasy that the adolescent has unusual capacities, such parental attitudes may stimulate the adolescent to become more megalomanic either by identification with his parents or out of his need to fulfill the enormous parental expectations. On the other hand, the adolescent who has achieved some success and has obtained some praise and recognition from his parents for his achievement and in addition has secured further ego information as to how to proceed in the direction of greater achievement, may then go on successfully without the need for megalomania.

As people grow into adulthood the normal course of events is that the adolescent megalomania becomes modified by the experience of reality. People discover through testing in real life experiences that they can accept limitations and at the same time achieve satisfaction to some degree. The adolescent whose megalomanic fantasies are intense and are not accompanied by constructive ego efforts tends, in treatment, to become dissatisfied with only a small amount of movement. This characteristic discontent with the amount of progress achieved is often a reflection of the adolescent's great expectations of what treatment will accomplish.

Present-day society stimulates megalomanic fantasies in adolescents. Part of the American dream is the idea that wishes can be fulfilled, that any individual can rise to great heights. The increased expectations of high schools today may also encourage megalomanic fantasies in certain adolescents, though at the same time, for others it may stimulate productivity. Some aspects of the culture play seductively into adolescent fantasies, as, for example, the enormous quick successes of young entertainers. It is easy for an adolescent to fantasy that he can become a great recording artist without studying music, or by further extension that he can become a great scientist without mastering the fundamentals of high school mathematics.

Therapeutically, megalomanic tendencies in adolescents are not discouraged unless this defense is extreme or bizarre. If the adolescent has a healthy ego, life will teach him the realistic limits. Even if his ego is weak, the counselor should be extremely cautious about discouraging hope since even with the pathological adolescent the megalomanic fantasies are restitutional efforts; attacking this defense might have serious effects if a substitute is not immediately available.

Whether adolescent megalomania turns out to be constructive or not depends on the manner in which the defense is used, whether the adolescent makes some realistic effort toward his goal or merely continues for a lengthy period in an unrealistic fantasy. If the overevaluation of his mental functioning is not extreme or persistent, this regression has value because it increases the adolescent's feeling of self-esteem. In spite of their megalomanic tendencies adolescents generally feel inadequate because of the reawakening of the oedipal conflict, among other factors. The regression to narcissism in its various manifestations sustains the adolescent through some of his difficulties by making him feel better.

In treatment, therefore, the counselor allows the adolescent to enjoy the heightened self-esteem which accompanies his megalomania, provided it is normal within the context of the *adolescent* world. The counselor should not deflate the ambitiousness of an adolescent who says he is writing a great novel. He should be tolerant of the fantasy element present and allow the adolescent to enjoy it for a while. This does not preclude reality-based comments to an adolescent when the counselor understands the normality of the adolescent narcissism and megalomanic tendencies.

The narcissism should never be deprecated because, especially with the talented or creative adolescent, from it ultimately may come valuable kinds of adult functioning. The counselor should gauge the capacity realistically and evaluate what the adolescent longs for in order to be able to consider in what measure the hopes can be realistically fulfilled. The adolescent should be helped to divert his energies into areas where he has capacity for production and in this way can be helped to adjust to reality.

The megalomanic hopes of adolescents may be threatening to parents. The parents' own hopes for fulfillment are reawakened more or less consciously and with discomfort by an adolescent. The parent is reminded that the adolescent has the high hopes, the self-involvement, the verve, that the adult has lost, or, that the adolescent may succeed in finding what the adult has never been able to capture. The barbed reminders may lead to depreciation by the adult of adolescent fantasies, or, in other cases, to overevaluation of the capacity of the adolescent with the concomitant pressures placed on the adolescent by parents hoping to achieve through their child.

There is a vulnerability in adolescents which is a source of concern to mature adults. Parents are aware that the adolescent may be hurt when he discovers the realities of the world as the adult knows them. Reality is not always pleasant or comfortable and adults are not always happy about their recognition of the realities. But an adult can be resigned and tolerant of situations that are not totally pleasing. Frequently parents see their own youthful fantasies aroused, old wounds reopened, old hopes re-awakened by an adolescent. This stirring of old feelings is pain-ful and is one of the major reasons why adults overreact to adolescents.

Another reason is that the adults who deal with adolescents, parents, teachers, counselors and others are aware that, more than at earlier periods, the adolescent has the capacity to make serious mistakes which may adversely affect his future. However adult concern may express itself, it is difficult if not impossible to convince adolescents of the limitations of reality or of their own ability, until their own experience forces recognition.

### 4. Philosophical Preoccupations

The adolescent preoccupation with his place in the universe is another manifestation of narcissism. Adolescents question their role in the universal scheme because they need to reorient themselves.

Reality provides meaning and boundaries for human experi-ence although everyone searches for meanings beyond reality. The adolescent looks for the ultimate purpose of life or the real meaning of existence, a search that is basically a groping for ultimate gratifications. The hope of achieving perfect gratifica-tion is illusory but human beings have the feeling that complete satisfaction exists somewhere if only it could be found. Folklore and myths confirm this universal search for the impossible per-fection, the Utopia, the gold at the end of the rainbow.

Probably the only time human beings approach this state of complete satisfaction is during infancy after a feeding. Perhaps this feeling that complete and ultimate satisfaction does exist is built into the human nervous system as a propelling force which maintains hopes. Whatever the source, human beings keep searching for the illusory goal of ultimate satisfaction. The human being is the insatiable animal.

The infant seeks complete gratification through fulfillment of the instinctual longings to be held, caressed and fed. The pubescent begins to think of this full satisfaction in terms of a perfect sexual relationship where the love object will be ultimately fulfilling. Adolescent fantasy always places this hope in the future. Only maturity is able to cope with the reality that ultimate fantasied gratification can never actually be achieved.

The adolescent search for ultimate meaning is a narcissistic preoccupation with perfect satisfactions and the means of achieving complete gratification. Regressions occur in this narcissistic preoccupation with self but these can be valuable for an adolescent. They may provide motivation for his future career, they may offer good sublimations of unsatisfied yearnings and they can enrich his mental life.

## Identification

The adolescent ego calls into play other adaptive mechanisms that alternate and fuse with earlier forms of mastery. One of the most striking and most characteristic is the process of identification. The adolescent wants to give up the persistent child in himself. Identification is the major technique by which he can achieve this. By identifying with adults who have resolved the numerous and complex problems of life (so far as the adolescent can judge) and who have achieved success in some area, he hopes to attain similar solutions for himself.

Identification is not new to the adolescent ego. It is a reinstatement of an ego mechanism which serves the growth process from infancy. Indeed, in adolescents it contains some of the original intense quality of the small child playing Daddy or Mommy. The identification of the adolescent still has an imitative histrionic quality that makes adults suspicious of his sincerity. Often the identification is resented by adults close to the adolescent who tell him to act his age. This is precisely what the adolescent does not want to do; he wants to act the adult's age. Adults are also amused when adolescents copy each other or irritated at times when the chosen model is a celebrity of whom the adult does not approve.

Often the parent is reacting to a caricature of himself reflected in his adolescent child. In the caricature he perceives his own faults and weaknesses and understandably this may be hard to take. If the parent has not himself resolved his conflicts (and this is usually true, at least to some degree) the identification with the parent will reveal one or another aspect of the forces in the conflict. The adolescent identifies with the very image which the parent has defended against or resolved; thus, the well-known instances of the minister's son who becomes a profligate or the atheist's son who becomes a minister.

Where hostility to the parent outweighs love, the identification may be hostile. The parent who is not loved may still be identified with, resulting often in self-hatred as well as hatred of the parent. Such identifications are seen in adolescents who struggle against their identities and who are unable to accept themselves.

It is important for the counselor to understand the process of identification and its proper guidance. Since it is a spontaneous unconscious process, identification will take place without encouragement, but because the adolescent ego sometimes makes identifications which do not benefit the personality, the counselor may need to redirect the identification toward more wholesome objects and contents.

The counselor will find himself an object of identification by the adolescent he is treating; when he expects this process he will not be surprised or made uncomfortable. He will accept his role as an identification figure and direct the identification in the way that will best suit the reality of the individual adolescent's potential. The values and behavior acquired through the process of identification become part of the ultimate character structure.

Almost always in adolescence there is some rebellion against the tendency to identify totally with the parents themselves. The identification is often displaced to extrafamilial figures, with the characteristic intensity, devotion and imitative quality of adolescents, resulting in the familiar hero worship and adolescent crush. The adolescent imitates his hero in appearance, and, so far as he is able, in action. He is preoccupied with thoughts and fantasies about his identification object down to the slightest details. The object for identification may be a movie star, a respected teacher or scout leader or a gangster. The choices are different but similar needs and mechanisms operate. The actual choice will reflect in some way, with or without conflict, the first object of identification, the parents.

If the parental relationship was relatively benign in the pre-adolescent years, then the adolescent, after his revolt, becomes more, rather than less, like his parents. As the child initially learned behavior out of love for his parents, and out of identification with them, so the adolescent learns again. Here lies a potent force for education and for treatment.

The adolescent also identifies with his teacher; the love and admiration he had for his parents, he now displaces onto teachers, especially if they are warm and interested. Adolescents who come from emotionally and culturally deprived homes particularly may profit from identification with a teacher. This process makes possible a change in important values which may make for an improved future.

## Withdrawal

Another adolescent regression takes the form of withdrawal from relationships for longer or shorter periods. The adolescents who use this defense seem happiest when they are by themselves, seem to have no need for others, and feel uncomfortable about social contacts or interaction with others. However their isolation does not have the lost affect of the withdrawn schizophrenic. Usually the withdrawal is a transient defense, a retreat before remobilization.

These periods of withdrawal provide a time for self-appraisal for some adolescents, a moratorium, to use Erikson's word, from which the adolescent may emerge with a more adaptive orientation. These periods may range in time from some small part of the day to months and may even extend to dropping out of school or other scheduled activities.

Parents and educators are sometimes alarmed by these withdrawals especially when they last more than a short time. Only careful diagnostic evaluation can determine the severity of the pathology involved and whether treatment is indicated. In most instances, the withdrawal will be transient.

### Regression to Homosexual Relationships

Adolescents frequently regress on a defensive and temporary basis to homosexual relationships. The adolescent uses this defense usually against both internal and external pressure toward heterosexuality. Commonly adolescents engage in some homosexual activity. Only if the choice of the love object remains homosexual is this pathological; when transient, it is an adolescent regression which can also be used for sexual experimentation. The adolescent tries to find out how to behave heterosexually by using a homosexual love object as if it were one of the opposite sex. When the homosexual relationships are sublimated, as in hero worship and crushes without sexuality, they can become the basis for valuable identifications on the part of the adolescent, for future career choices and for healthy character traits.

### Asceticism

Asceticism is an attempt to deny any expression of an unacceptable impulse, usually sexuality. It inhibits discharge of the impulse and avoids involvement in the relationship which would give rise to the impulse.

Commonly, ascetic adolescents are not conscious of their impulses and so repression also operates. There are however ascetics who are conscious of their impulses and inhibit, suppress, or at times simply endure the frustration of the impulses. Defenses such as rationalization, reaction formation and denial are also involved in asceticism. Certain countercathexes are sometimes used in asceticism in which the person feels negative affect such as disgust and revulsion against the impulse. The ego may also use processes such as social withdrawal to avoid situations which stimulate the impulse.

Adolescents are more prone to adopt asceticism defensively than adults. There is an intensity about asceticism which has an adolescent quality. Much energy is thrown into it as a defensive system. For most adolescents the asceticism is transient but at the time it occurs they may be more intensely ascetic than adults. The adolescent ego becomes overwhelmed by impulse periodically and then the defense rises again. It is not uncommon for adolescents to swing from episodes of sexual acting out to vows of life-long chastity and back to sexuality when the impulses break through.

## Contradictory Strivings for Dependence and Independence

The demand for gratification is always strong in adolescents. The dependency needs for warmth, physical closeness, support and protection, which originally were gratified by the parents, now must be found in other relationships. The adolescent also has to satisfy himself from within. The dependent needs remain, but the adolescent struggles with the maturational pull towards independence, so that the needs are mutually exclusive and create conflict. The adolescent regresses to childish behavior, then is impelled to assert independence and be an adult. Granted independence, he becomes fearful and his behavior reveals the longings for dependence. For example, a boy may demand the right to stay out as late as he pleases without parental controls, but while he is out he will telephone home to let his parents know where he is and when to expect him. Adolescent girls often insist on the adult right to shop for clothes without their mothers' supervision but may also expect their mothers to keep their clothing laundered and their rooms in order.

Counselors should make use of the dependent needs of adolescents. The adolescent can allow a counselor to meet some of his dependency needs while he still retains the wish for independence. He maintains his façade of independence at the same time that he leans on the counselor. And the counselor can permit the adolescent to be dependent while he helps the adolescent achieve independence. The adolescent may deny dependent needs when he is at home, yet be able to express his longings for his parents openly to his counselor. The ego ideal of the adolescent is one of complete independence and he will usually be ashamed to face how dependent he really is or wants to be. The counselor can use the dependency needs to help the treatment process, not by confronting the adolescent with his dependent yearnings, but by allowing dependency while encouraging the wish to be independent. The dependent longings are satisfied by having the counselor encourage the adolescent to feel that he accepts the adolescent's wish to be independent now and ultimately.

# 5

# Other Ego Adaptations and Defenses

THE WAY IN WHICH adolescents use defenses ultimately produces a defensive picture that appears qualitatively and quantitatively different from the defense structure of other age groups, but the defenses themselves are the same. There is no defense that is exclusive to adolescents. However, the nature of adolescent development modifies the defenses or produces a conglomeration of defenses unique to adolescents.

Generally the purpose of adult defenses is protection against internal conflict; adolescents defend themselves from inner conflicts, but they also use defenses in the actual interaction between themselves and the important people in their lives. Outside influences are still important in affecting the defensive structure of adolescents, while in adults the inner personality structure plays the greater part. As the adolescent approaches adulthood character becomes crystallized and a selected number of typical defenses is settled upon and used more consistently.

Defensive structures are complex and individual but it is possible to highlight general characteristics which differentiate adolescent use of defenses from that of adults:

The intensity with which a defense is used is greater in the adolescent than in adults. The intensity of adolescent life is greater in all ego functioning including the defenses.

Defenses are more transient in adolescents, more persistent in adults.

The adolescent tends to use a wider variety of different defenses, the adult settles for fewer.

The adolescent is more flexible in his use of defenses because he does not have the usage totally integrated. The adult's use of defenses is part of a total and persistent character structure.

Parents, other adults, including the celebrities of the sports and entertainment world, peers, and beginning heterosexual relationships help to influence adolescent defenses while inner motivations are the determining factors for an adult.

Adolescents need to be like others in their peer group while an adult can bear to be himself. The adolescent is so anxious not to be different that he may be motivated to alter his defenses. The adolescent adopts superficial defenses almost voluntarily because of peer pressure rather than out of inner needs.

The realization that time is passing is a significant motivation for change in an adult. The feeling that life is moving on rapidly does not exercise enough pressure for an adolescent to feel the need to modify his defenses or adapt differently.

In the adolescent the concept that reality can be changed to suit one's self is strong (magical thinking) but an adult realizes the nature of reality and its limitations.

Hope of fulfillment is so intense in adolescents that it becomes a motivating factor for behavior, and the high degree of hope makes it possible for him to postpone any alteration of maladaptive defenses. An adult is more realistic and knows that he must make efforts to obtain gratification.

Ego adaptations are usually thought of as benign while defenses are considered pathological. But adaptation consists of any kind of behavior which makes it possible for an individual to function with a minimum of inner pain. And defenses can be benign. They are clinically significant only when the behavior resulting from their use causes personal unhappiness or harm in the environment.

When an impulse can be discharged directly there is no need for a defensive structure. For example when a person has the impulse to eat, is conscious of his impulse and has food available, he may satisfy the impulse directly and simply by eating. But if the impulse is to eat food forbidden by his culture or religion, as for instance, pork if he is an orthodox Jew or a Mohammedan, then he must erect defenses to deal with his impulse.

Defenses arise as protection against danger. Their function is the same for the ego as for a threatened nation. Psychological defenses are special kinds of ego adaptions for the purpose of guarding against discomfort from either inner or outer stress.

Human beings defend themselves in many ways. There are physiological defenses in the structure of the body for defense against bacteria. Although it is obvious that the physiological defenses against disease are innate and not learned, it is not so obvious that people are born with psychological defenses. But it is conceptually valid to assume that the human organism constitutionally has the capacity for developing certain defenses, while others are learned from the environment.

It is difficult to determine whether the defense mechanisms are innate or acquired because incorporation and identification occur early in life and these are the bases for acquiring many defenses. For example, compulsive parents may make a conscious effort to be undemanding about toilet training. Still at the age of a year and one-half their untrained child may already have compulsive mannerisms. The question then arises whether the child had a constitutional propensity for compulsivity or whether incorporation of and identification with compulsive parents took place early in his life.

Defenses may also be self-learned, not necessarily as a result of trauma. Many modern parents have relaxed attitudes about sex, yet children continue to feel guilty about masturbation. A child has a limited ego span and interprets and reacts on the basis of his own narrow experience which can result in self-induced conflict. The ego integrative capacities come out of ego maturation.

Any psychological or physical phenomenon which implies direct or indirect danger, the reality of an oncoming automobile or the perception of an unpleasant sensation motivates defenses. Even conscious management of impulse has defensive aspects. Whether conscious or unconscious, defenses are ego adaptations. The ego would be unable to function if it were flooded with every impulse from within or every stimulus from without. An ego defense is that type of adaptation which tries to protect the organization of the personality against painful or disintegrative psychic processes, but defenses are also used against painful and dangerous aspects of external reality. They may be directed against anything which might create stress in the organism.

Defenses are usually not used singly. They ordinarily appear in combination with other ego adaptations or modes of handling impulses. An inhibited boy may show no signs of anger or sexual feeling. He may have a general defense of inhibition against impulses and affects in which a number of specific defenses are being used: among them, projection, repression, blocking of affect and reaction formation.

It is important to differentiate between defenses and characterological attitudes; attitude is a conscious affective orientation. A boy who says he does not believe people should fight may not be defending against his own impulse to be angry. He may believe that a person should be angry at certain appropriate times, may consciously feel angry and acknowledge his anger, but he holds the attitude that fighting is wrong. Neither blocking nor denial of affect is involved.

Individuals vary greatly in their capacity to tolerate anxiety or to endure difficult realities. Some people are able to endure much internal anxiety; some can face difficult external reality without the necessity of defending themselves by changing the nature of their perception of reality. The quality and quantity of the defensive structure is therefore a consideration in personality assessment.

Human beings are highly complex and each individual has a unique history. Therefore each person can develop systems of defense which are characteristic for himself alone. In order to clarify diagnostic concepts, classification of defenses is attempted but in actual life people use defenses that cannot be simply described. A person maintains defenses because he has found, through his own unique experience, that some particular kind of defensive system functions for him. A description of an episode in the life of an individual, in narrative form, may better characterize that individual than a catalogue of his defenses.

The following defenses are seen frequently and significantly in adolescent character structure.

## Impulse Gratification as Defense

All impulses exist for the purpose of biological and psychological survival. Satisfying an impulse directly is highly gratifying and the organism is driven to obtain that gratification.

In infancy most impulses are satisfied with minimal ego activity but as a child grows, and development progresses, the environment no longer provides gratification passively and the ego has to become involved in some activity in order to secure gratification.

The direction of personality development lies in this change from gratification by passive modes to gratification by means of the ego's active participation. When an impulse cannot be gratified frustration arises and then the ego acts to prevent this frustration. The ego may repress the impulse in order to defend against the frustration in an effort to stop the clamor for gratification, and other ego functions handle the state of non-gratification, the superego, awareness of the external environment, and consideration of consequences.

In adolescence there is a resurgence and intensification of impulses. The ego, put under pressure to gratify them, may do so directly and actively. The pressures in such a situation are great and the adolescent ego has not yet accrued sufficient other considerations to resist.

Direct impulse gratification ordinarily is an ego adaptation but it may be defensive if one impulse is gratified to defend against another impulse which is not acceptable.

Some adolescents become so anxious and guilty over various impulses, particularly sexuality and aggressiveness, that they gratify, not these, but other impulses. They act out by stealing, cheating or gang delinquencies because these activities help to relieve the tension of the conflict and the affects of guilt and shame over basic sexuality and aggressiveness. An adolescent might find it unacceptable to be aggressive against a parent, but permissible to discharge the aggression when the object is changed to a teacher in school, by undesirable behavior, or to the community by the act of stealing.

Direct impulse gratification may also be a defense against the more infantile dependent impulses that cannot realistically be completely satisfied. The impulse is insatiable and the individual tries to get gratification from, for instance, gambling or stealing.

Adolescents may seek impulse gratification to distract themselves from the various conflicts and anxieties with which they cannot deal directly. They may have no satisfaction from their school work or they may feel unsettled about their goals; family

life may be intolerable; they may be confused about their identities. Impulse gratifications in the experiences of marijuana
"kicks," LSD "trips," alcoholic highs, orgiastic sex, and destructive escapades serve the defensive function of distracting them
from the troubles of the adolescent life struggle.

There are different implications for treatment when the direct
gratification is defensive and when it is not. If direct acting on
impulse is not defensive, the ego is one that insists on gratification and is unable to withhold against the pressures of an impulse. Treatment, then, should be directed, not to uncovering,
but to educating the ego to add to its capacity to withstand
impulse.

When direct gratification is used defensively the treatment
should be directed not to the activity but to what is going on
dynamically. Not uncommonly adolescents are seen in treatment
who appear to be without superegos. They quarrel with their
parents and are difficult disciplinary problems at school. Sometimes these adolescents are irritable, or brashly defiant. In treatment they may be insolent and unresponsive.

But if the counselor can overcome his countertransference—
and this kind of adolescent is sometimes extremely hard to take
—he may discover that what appears as a delinquent character
formation is a manifestation of impulse gratification as a denial
of the force of a primitive superego, a defensive structure against
a serious depression.

### Undirected Motor Activity

Undirected motor activity is a discharge phenomenon without
specific goal direction and ego integration. Adolescents often
engage in either random or rhythmic physical activities such as
rocking, swaying, kicking, or tapping. This undirected motor
activity is different from sublimation or displacement. One of its
primary characteristics descriptively is that it is transient. It is

a series of activities none of which need be a regular part of the individual's total behavior pattern. The quality of randomness is what is characteristic along with the motor component.

In its widest sense undirected motor activity is an ego adaptation but it may have a defensive aspect. If an adolescent is sexually tense, but cannot have direct sexual gratification, he may engage in random physical activity, as a way of discharging tensions. The advice frequently given to sexually tense adolescents to "run around the block" is based on the recognition that motor activity can discharge tension. Some adolescents find relief only after exhausting themselves physically. These motor activities are not engaged in for the intrinsic pleasure of the athletics, which would be a sublimation.

## DISPLACEMENT

Displacement is an attempt on the part of the ego to prevent awareness of the source of an impulse. Some parts of the body are readily associated in the unconscious with other parts that have some physical similarity, as for example, the penis and the nose. The fantasy of excitement in the penis may be repressed and the source displaced to the nose; the individual then experiences concern about the nose; there may be new attitudes about the nose. Such a displacement also involves symbolization.

In boys, concern about the nose is usually a concern about the adequacy of the penis. Girls have more interest in their total appearance and attractiveness and their worry about the size and shape of their noses is less specifically sexual. For this reason, adolescent boys who want plastic surgery on the nose may be more disturbed emotionally than girls who wish cosmetic surgery. But girls who are concerned about their own bi-sexuality and penis envy may also displace onto the nose.

The ear and the inside of the nose can symbolize the anus; both have the anal characteristics of body openings which discharge objectionable secretions. Anal picking may be displaced to nose, ear, skin and nail picking. The repressed impulses in these cases have to do with the anal products, feces.

Hair on the head is a ready symbol for pubic hair even before pubescence. Adolescent boys commonly tease each other by saying that hair will grow on the palms of the hands if they masturbate. Because of its association with the genitalia, hair in general has sexual significance.

Long hair is usually equated with femininity. The current fad for long hair among adolescent boys, though perhaps stimulated by the success of the Beatles, may be an expression of the concern about their sexual identity. Both boys and girls protest that long hair makes boys look more manly and more mature; they cite historical precedent for this opinion from Samson to the Cavaliers. Their parents, however, sensing the unconscious sexual symbolization, frequently overreact to what they consider dirtiness or perversity.

## PROJECTION

In projection, if the repressed tends to come into consciousness, the ego blames someone or something outside of itself for the unacceptable impulse or attitude. Projection manifests itself in blaming others and suspecting the thoughts of others. It is also manifest in the externalization of inner perceptions as in hallucinations in which a disturbing inner experience is actually perceived as belonging to the outside world.

Projection occurs universally; everyone tends to find faults in others. It is pathological only when there is insufficient basis in reality to accord with the projection.

Adolescents use projection frequently, finding fault with and throwing blame on their teachers, parents and others, at times of inner stress. Adolescents are reluctant to recognize that they themselves are responsible for any of their difficulties; they rationalize their own behavior and blame others for the consequences. They are sensitive to the most minute idiosyncrasies and deviations in their parents and their peers and project their own faults onto those shortcomings in others.

## PROVOCATION

Provocation is a form of acting out by the use of behavior which has the intention of causing a reaction, usually hostile, in another person. Out of his own need, the provoking adolescent tries to arouse a hostile reaction from the object of his provocation. The provocation serves many purposes and is not always fully conscious, especially in masochistic adolescents, but ordinarily the aggressive impulse and the management of hostility are involved.

Often the purpose of provocation is to alleviate guilt resulting from hostile and destructive impulses. The provoker acts in a way that brings a hostile response. The resulting punishment alleviates the guilt so that the provoker will often feel better once he has been punished. This particular dynamic is common in sado-masochistic relationships. It is also common with adolescents who discover how to tease and provoke parents and others, particularly with actions that in themselves do not seem serious or hostile. Not hearing when spoken to, persistent humming, tapping fingers or kicking feet and grimacing, are examples of ordinary kinds of provocation which adolescents frequently use.

Whether behavior is provocative or not depends in part on how the person being provoked interprets that behavior. Adolescents may not always be provocative merely because their actions cause another individual to become irritated or angered. The important aspect is the intent, usually unconscious, of the person who does the provoking. However, with adolescents, most behavior which is felt by others to be provocative actually does have that intention. Adolescents have a particularly acute sense about what will be most upsetting to their parents, even if the parents attempt to control their feelings. The adolescent senses how the parents are reacting inwardly.

Provocation is a common adolescent defense and a difficult one to treat because it arouses hostility rather than sympathy on the part of the provoked person. The adolescent can often deny the hostility inherent in his provocation and appear to be innocent of any wrongdoing serious enough to merit extreme hostile reaction. He frequently responds with martyred looks and a puzzled "Who, me?" or a bland "What did I do?" which are actually further subtle provocation.

It is not usually helpful for a counselor to advise parents not to react to adolescent provocation since this is almost impossible to achieve because of the subtlety of the adolescent provocation and the adolescent's awareness of inner reaction even when the parent is trying to maintain control. However, since part of the purpose of the provocation is to get the parent to lose control, if the parent can hold out long enough, maintain sufficient control to ignore some particular piece of behavior, that particular provocation may cease. Time itself is on the side of the parents since as adolescents mature provocative behavior usually lessens. When parents do react to provocations the adolescent is accomplishing what he meant to accomplish; if controls firm enough can be established by the parent, the provocation will be given up and some other type of behavior, perhaps more tolerable, will be substituted. The difficulty for teachers, parents and others lies, however, in the uncanny ability of the adolescent to sense what will be most disturbing to them and to use different but equally annoying behavior with different people.

Provocation may also take the form of wedging, a technique for expressing hostility or of gaining one's own way through creating interference in the relationship of others. Common adolescent examples of this technique are reporting the wrongdoings of siblings to parents, playing off one parent against the other either to gain favor from one or to get them to be hostile to each other.

## COUNTERPHOBIA

The counterphobic defense is one in which an individual performs an act or allows himself to feel an affect of which he is afraid. Counterphobia involves a kind of unconscious rationalization. The ego, in effect, says, "See, there is nothing here to be afraid of really; I can do it." The ego gives reassurance through the rationalization and through engaging in the impulse or the affect which is feared.

The counterphobic defense may be expressed consciously but it still makes use of unconscious mechanisms; evaluation goes on in the ego at deeper levels. Sometimes athletic prowess in adolescents originates in fear and is developed through counterphobic measures. A boy who is afraid of the diving board may feel it is shameful to be afraid and therefore forces himself to dive from the highest board. He is compelled to perform the feared act; because the anxiety is not always relieved, the act must be repeated. The repetition comes out of the ego's persistent need to solve a conflict when a situation occurs which rearouses the conflict.

Unlike reaction formation, the counterphobic defense does not require doing the opposite of what is feared. The counterphobic individual engages in the very act or experience which he fears. In response to hostile impulses, the person with reaction formation becomes kind, loving and ingratiating, while the counterphobic expresses his hostility, although both have anxiety about hostility.

The anxiety in the counterphobic individual is frequently obvious. An adolescent girl, frightened of sexuality, may throw herself wildly at boys to prove that she is not afraid. Her anxiety is evident but she would be more uneasy and unhappy if she did not run after boys. Most counterphobic mechanisms require rationalizations and denial of the amount of danger involved. Other motivations besides anxiety also push the ego to engage in feared acts, such as shame, the desire to prove something or the need to earn money.

Any one bit of behavior may have various dynamics and different defenses may operate to produce the manifest behavior. A boy who fears aggressive physical contact may develop into a good football player out of counterphobic defense but he may also be acting out of fear of hostility and competition, out of castration anxiety or fear of feminine identification.

Genital sexuality is new to adolescents; all are anxious about it. Most adolescents begin to date in spite of anxiety and learn out of the experience that dating is not as dangerous as they had feared. The adolescent with great sexual anxiety may date counterphobically. For some adolescents this counterphobic action results in relief of the fears and anxiety; in others the anxiety may continue and their heterosexual experiences may be counterphobic over an extended period of time.

Everyone uses some counterphobic mechanisms because everyone has fears, realistically related to the anxieties of de-velopment, or unrealistic, but for several reasons counterphobic mechanisms are seen more commonly in adolescents than in adults. Adults usually are not ashamed or afraid to admit when they are afraid. Life experience has taught them to make peace with their own shortcomings. They know that other adults also have fears and they have acquired many ways of disguising anxiety.

An adolescent is less ready than an adult to admit his fears. He hates to acknowledge his weaknesses, feels he must prove he is adequate. An adolescent may acknowledge that he is afraid to his counselor but not to his peers. To be considered chicken is intolerable and adolescents will engage in dangerous acts of a counterphobic nature. These counterphobic acts may even appear suicidal although the psychological intent is different. The counterphobic act is death-defying rather than death-seeking.

To meet the developmental tasks required of him the adolescent must act in the face of fears. Experience will relieve most adolescents of their anxiety and they will eventually not need to act counterphobically. But if there are deep unconscious anxieties, the counterphobic mechanism will continue. The more unconscious the issue, the more entangled in the past, the greater will be the anxiety and the need to defend the self. A fear arising out of the present will be more easily relieved.

## OVERCOMPENSATION

Similar to counterphobia is overcompensation, where a particular capacity is used excessively, perhaps to prove something, but not out of fear of the act itself. A boy may exercise constantly with dumbbells to develop his muscles because he is ashamed of being weak.

Adolescents use overcompensation frequently. They suffer so much from feelings of physical inadequacy as well as intellectual inferiority, emotional conflict and ignorance of life that they try to overcome these feelings by an exaggeration of the kind of behavior which they think will counter the impression they would otherwise create. Overcompensation accounts for the frequent boasting of adolescents, their superciliousness, their pseudo-sophistication and even for their excessive dedication to athletics, the arts and, occasionally, to school work.

Adolescent girls, in their desire to be popular and accepted, may overcompensate by being excessively involved in dating, sometimes to the extent of promiscuity.

## EXHIBITIONISM

Exhibitionism is an ego mechanism for affecting the onlooker but it is not an exaggeration of affect or behavior like dramatization. It may be as undramatic as a show of nonchalance. Exhibitionism is a defense based on awareness that reality is not what one would wish it to be; therefore the exhibitionist does something out of the ordinary to create an effect, or he plays some role to win over others.

Exhibitionism involves engaging in a show whether it takes the form of wearing a uniform or of displaying genitalia. Basically the exhibitionist is concerned with and suffers from shame. The shame may relate to bodily inadequacy or to a feeling that others will reject or make fun of what he actually has to display. It is an attempt to overcome negative reaction by showing something positive.

Exhibitionism is almost universal in some phases of adolescence because adolescents suffer from shame, inferiority and inadequacy feelings. Adolescent exhibitionism accounts for much of the behavior and the hair and clothing styles which adults frequently criticize; it accounts also for tough, wise guy or big shot behavior and offensive loudness and disorderliness in public places. Many types of exhibitionism are sanctioned by peers and a whole group of adolescents will act and dress exhibitionistically. Individual exhibitionism, without peer sanctions, however, is thought of as queer, and is unacceptable to adolescents.

## CLOWNING

Clowning is a complex acting out behavior in an attempt to affect others. The clowning adolescent endeavors to remove the seriousness of his feelings, to be playful rather than to reveal the actual impulses or conflicts, in order to avoid the possibility of negative reaction. Sometimes when the superego dictates that the impulses would be unacceptable the behavior is modified to clowning in order that the impulse may became benign instead of hostile. Clowning is expected to amuse, not arouse anger, and to avoid the retaliation which might otherwise come.

The clowning of young or latency age children, which often appears as a silly burst of activity, represents a random relief of anxiety so poorly directed by the ego that the observer can get little meaning from it. In young adolescents clowning may be an attention getting device. The clowning of younger adolescents seems less purposeful and more undifferentiated than in older adolescents where the specific purpose and underlying emotional issues behind the clowning behavior are often discernible.

The specific type of clowning may reveal what the impulse is and in this sense the defense of clowning is counterphobic. For instance, almost universally young adolescent boys act silly in front of girls and tease them. The sexual impulses are present but boys are not ready to reveal them seriously and can only play at sexuality.

Adolescents may clown to be provocative and to express hostility. Clowning in the classroom frequently has this aspect. The delinquent gang may have a clown who can act hostilely toward the leader without retaliation because of the amusing nature of his behavior. This is the traditional role of the court jester.

Clowning may be used as a defense against depression, an attempt to lighten the gravity of the hostility, to lessen the profundity of the inner suffering. In this use clowning acts as a defense against impulses directed toward internalized objects.

Clowning is generally unacceptable for adults and when used is seen as appropriate only temporarily and at restricted times. An adult may act the clown in some social situations while he realizes that clowning is inappropriate to his usual personality. Adolescents will use clowning more persistently and for them it may be more of a counterphobic mechanism. In adults clowning may be connected with underlying depressive feelings while in adolescents, it is usually concerned with affecting others. Professional clowns or comedians are frequently depressed people.

Certain types of clowning, sarcastic witticisms or cynical mimicry involve conscious decisions about the kind of action to perform. At the highest level of clowning the adult professional comedian must engage in conscious ego activity to prepare his material and put his clowning into effect.

Adolescents use clowning more than adults because adolescents take to action. At any age boys are more given to clowning than girls, who may express somewhat similar attitudes by giggling. However, outbursts of giggling in girls are more related to internalized feelings, an effort to relieve tension or embarrassment, and are less concerned with affecting the relationship to others.

## Superego Corruption

The adolescent superego is not as completely consolidated as that of the adult. Consequently the adolescent seems at times to have a corrupt superego. The superego indicates a particular way to handle an impulse; the adolescent ego may not go along with the superego's dictates and the superego yields. But in order for corruption to occur, superego values must exist, with the ego behaving contrary to the internal values. In adolescence what appears to be corruption may take place as a consequence of rebellion against the parental superego standards or as part of the adolescent's testing of his own superego values.

A student who knows it is wrong to cheat on an examination will feel guilty if he does cheat. But when he cheats, he gives indication of a corruptible superego which is not strong enough to deter the wrongdoing. The superego may be influenced by outside pressures; "everybody" is cheating. The superego almost always permits some influencing from outside as well as from inner pressures; an adolescent who never yields to outside pressures would be uncomfortable with a pathologically rigid superego.

Some behavior can be rationalized. The superego is put aside temporarily, to avoid the pain of guilt, and later reinstated. A student who would not permit himself to cheat on an examination in mathematics might cheat without guilt on a test in physical education which he does not consider important. Certain issues have many superego considerations and others, which do not, are more easily rationalized.

One of the criteria for differentiating the adult from the

adolescent is whether or not superego values are firmly established. Since the adolescent ego has not yet settled what the permanent superego values will be, adolescents can yield to certain kinds of behavior without guilt more easily than adults. With strong impulses and unsettled superego values, the adolescent therefore will vary considerably in his attitudes toward the same issue. The adult sorts out certain values to which he attaches real significance. The fluctuation seen in adolescents is characteristic of their mode of handling certain impulses in relation to the superego. In adulthood, and in latency, for different reasons there is much more consistency in the superego. Also the latency child may fear the consequences of giving in to impulses contrary to the superego more than the adolescent does, and therefore his behavior is more constant.

If the adolescent's own superego allows him to go against its edicts, he may try to get others to go along with him since adolescents love company and need support from their peers. This may involve a process of corrupting others.

### Altruism

Altruism is a complex ego adaptation for the purpose of handling relationships. The ego acts in a benign manner, seems to be oriented to the welfare of others but like all behavior, its roots lie in self-interest. Altruism may be defensive or non-defensive. As a defense altruism may be directed against selfishness, a direct defense against impulse. Whether it is a good or harmful defense depends on how the ego adaptation is structured, how it is overtly used and what internal forces are operating.

Pure altruism of a non-defensive nature is almost never seen clinically. The altruist shows interest in others, is not overly preoccupied with himself, will sacrifice his own comfort for others without going to the extremes of harming himself. Consciously such a person feels gratification in this behavior and may not see any selfishness or enlightened self-interest in what he does.

Dynamically this development arises from early experiences with a giving person, usually the mother. The child then identifies himself with this other person, wants to be like her and give to her as he has been given to. True altruism is approached when the affect of having been given to is unconscious and the conscious pleasure is in being like the giving person.

Non-defensive altruism may also be based on consciously remembering how good the mother was and consciously wanting to be like her. What is remembered is the identification, not the specific experiences of having received. An individual must have had the experience of being given to for non-defensive altruism to develop.

All mature people have some degree of altruism, although complete altruism is never possible. The concept of healthy normality however includes some degree of doing for others.

Altruism may not be motivated by actual self-interest but secondarily self-interest accrues from it because the altruistic feeling is self-fulfilling. Excessive altruism as a defense is seen in those individuals who need to bind others to them by their own need to be needed.

When adolescents use the defense of altruism it is likely to be extreme. Probably at no other period in life are people so altruistic and at the same time so self-centered as in adolescence. Adults generally admire altruism and the altruistic adolescent may receive praise and be held up as an example. But the altruistic adolescent may not get along with his peers, may be taken advantage of by them, or be ridiculed.

### SUBLIMATION

Sublimation is an ego mechanism which is not usually considered defensive. It is a benign discharge or gratification of impulses which when carefully examined always has some defensive components. Conflict is involved in all sublimation to some degree. The source of the impulse, the impulse itself, the mode of discharge, the object, any or all of these may be altered out of conflict and the alteration is defensive in purpose. Because most sublimations involve complex and highly organized ego functions, their ego-adaptive nature is most often emphasized while the defensive mechanisms with the aspect of conflict resolution are not as often recognized.

For example, an adolescent describes that he feels depressed, distressed and preoccupied. He is not sure what the feelings are but he knows that he gets relief if he plays the piano. A conflict is present with tension. Resolution is necessary and the sublimation of music provides that resolution of conflict and a benign discharge of impulse. However, not all creativity is the result of conflict.

Creative individuals who enter treatment often wonder if it will interfere with their ability to sublimate and therefore hinder the productive and creative use of their talent. Usually, however, a creative but conflicted individual will be better able to use his gifts after treatment. If the inclination was toward the use of creative sublimation, after resolution of conflict he will be more, rather than less, creative.

It is possible, however, for a person to have pseudo-sublimation. For example, an adolescent girl with neither real creative talent nor artistic energy paints because this fits her concept of a fashionable intellectual. She is not really compelled to express herself creatively or to use artistic sublimation in the way that truly creative people are. A pseudo-creative person may decrease his investment in the sublimation as he becomes emotionally healthier through treatment.

In treating adolescents counselors should not interfere with or interpret sublimations. Occasionally it may be necessary to control the exaggerated aspects of unrealistic sublimations or try to modify them, but generally sublimations are encouraged. Sublimations are important ego adaptations for adolescents and should be fostered. Sublimations develop during latency and adolescence because the ego has a large repertoire of defenses on which to draw out of the psychic content and experiences from the past. In adolescence the loosening of the character structure, the available energy and the physical maturation make this the period when the creativity implicit in satisfying sublimations is discovered if it is ever going to occur.

While in general counselors encourage sublimations in adolescents, reality problems sometimes intervene. An adolescent who wants to be a musician cannot spend his days practicing even if he has great talent. The law forces him to attend school whether or not he is interested in the ordinary educational routine. Adults have more freedom to change the realities of their lives; they can change careers, change families through divorce, or change their physical environment by moving. Adolescents cannot always freely pursue their sublimations. And sometimes the sublimations do not find approval in the eyes of parents and others thus creating further obstacles.

If there is real talent it may be tragic to interfere with the adolescent's ambition in these directions. Even if the talent is only average or minimal it may be better to allow the adolescent to discover his limitations for himself. Interference with sublimations also interferes with the character equilibrium and with the hope of fulfillment in life.

Where there is no talent or opportunity for fulfillment it may be necessary to treat the sublimation as a symptom and analyze its components. Sometimes this cannot be achieved until the adolescent is older and more realistic about himself. Many sublimation activities lose their hold on adolescents as they reach adulthood. Unfortunately the promise of creativity in youth is not often fulfilled and sublimations are frequently lost from the personalities of talented and capable adolescents as well as from those without talents.

An adolescent comes into treatment with his own individual defensive structure which the counselor must evaluate in terms of how and why the defenses are being used and whether they function effectively. No defense is attacked. The counselor will reinforce good defenses, those that are performing their function of making the adolescent more comfortable with himself and that do not cause difficulties in his environment. Hopefully, in the course of treatment, defenses that do not work, that fail of their protective purpose, will yield to more satisfactory modes of handling impulses, perceptions, affects and relationships.

# 6

# Engaging the Adolescent in Treatment

MANY KINDS of adolescent maladjustment and malfunctioning are tolerated or ignored over an extended period before serious attempts at treatment are started. Parents often hope that time will act as a cure. They expected some changes to occur in their children with the onset of adolescence and frequently cannot distinguish between transitory normal adolescent behavior and more permanently disabling personality characteristics and malfunction.

In school, too, problems are most often first handled by routine disciplinary methods such as withdrawal of privileges, extra assignments or lowered grades. Even those schools that have counselors available usually need to reserve their time for problems which have not yielded to handling by classroom teachers.

If the problems continue other measures become necessary, and the next attempts are usually of a manipulative or environmental nature. Parents set up rules which they try to enforce consistently. They try a change of school for educational problems or new recreational outlets for the adolescent when they disapprove of his associates and activities or when they are worried about his lack of friends and interests. They may consult a physician or clinic for physical examination. Some parents join groups aimed at improving family relations in order to learn how to handle the problems.

Often these efforts at home and at school give good results. The additional attention, the changes in parental management, shifts in school or in curriculum, and the development of new interests may serve to meet the adolescent's needs. But when the problems lie in the adolescent's character structure a different approach may be needed to effect improvement.

The adolescents who are referred to an agency for treatment are those who have not benefited from other helping methods. Adolescents seldom seek out help on their own and indeed, both they and their parents may be doubtful about the efficacy of still another form of help. Parents often say in a hopeless kind of way, "We've tried everything." The adolescent may be fearful about any kind of treatment that he identifies as headshrinking, or he may be resentful, apathetic, or anxious about the prospect of talking to or being talked at by one more adult.

The counselor who understands the characteristics of the adolescent personality knows that the helping techniques must differ from those used with adults or with younger children. An adolescent cannot tolerate the demands, often frustrating, of adult treatment, nor would he respond if he were placed in the role of a child. Effective treatment is tailored to fit the inconsistencies, the flexibility, the resilience and the hunger for understanding almost universal in adolescents.

The adolescent personality usually is not completely formed and pathology is not entrenched. The adolescent is susceptible to influence, direction and modification of behavior. He has an increased supply of energy available for solution of conflicts. Adolescents have intense need for identification with extrafamilial figures; they need an ally to help them find their way into the world of adults. The dangers of independence are great and so is the need for protection. Adolescents hunger for someone who will guard and guide them through the circuitous twist-ings of their own shifting behavior and feelings; they will accept this strength, guidance and security from an adult who under-stands and likes them.

The chief positive element in treatment is the adolescent's strong need for relationship. He is searching for an ego ideal; he will probably wish to identify with his counselor. The entire treatment hinges upon the establishment of a strong dependent relationship and the beginning of treatment should be devoted to building this relationship as the foundation for treatment.

No one single treatment technique will serve all adolescents. Each must be treated in accordance with individual needs based on individual diagnosis. Every type of technique from purely environmental to insight may be employed and it is not unusual that all techniques may be necessary at different times during the treatment of any one adolescent. Supportive and ego building techniques are always necessary in all stages of treatment with adolescents but are vital in the early phase.

In general, the treatment goals are oriented toward expanding ego capacity in two ways: by reduction of environmental dis-abilities, and by alleviation of emotional problems. The objec-tives are to help the adolescent achieve a higher level of function-ing and a greater use of ego capacity and energy, a lessening of symptoms, a structuring of defenses which will control anxiety and impulses, and a reasonable degree of comfort in workable relationships with parents, friends and others.

Synthesis, not analysis, is the essential goal. The treatment is directed toward synthesis of the innumerable issues in the life of the adolescent; it deals with the conscious ego but is absorbed by the unconscious.

From parents, school, and all other available sources, in-cluding medical examinations to rule out physical and organic pathology, the counselor should gather as much information as it is possible to obtain relating to the present and past of the individual adolescent. The more detailed and relevant this history material is, the more easily he will be able to prepare a tentative diagnostic formulation which leads to his choice of an initial approach that will be most suitable for the specific adolescent. This preliminary planning is essential in order to establish an atmosphere that removes some of the adolescent's apprehensions and meets some of his immediate needs.

In approaching the treatment of an adolescent, his actual behavior, however unacceptable or bizarre, or the symptoms which bring him into treatment, are of less importance than appraisal of his basic ego strengths. Whatever the fluctuations and complexities of his feelings and behavior, if the counselor can sense integrity of the ego, the ultimate prognosis is likely to be favorable.

The following are prognostic criteria which should be carefully examined no matter how serious or disturbed the symptomatic behavior appears:

Is the overall trend of character formation in the direction of maturity, regardless of the starting point and the temporary regressions? Has he settled on predominantly infantile modes of adjustment or does he seem motivated to grow up?

Is the adolescent attempting to deal with his complex problems in an effort to achieve some kind of integration or does he seem overwhelmed by them?

Is he still in the process of change or are the characteristic flexibility and resourcefulness of the adolescent ego missing? Are his difficulties chronic and persistent?

Is there active conflict, guilt and anxiety over unacceptable behavior or have the difficulties been pathologically solidified?

Does he have a good ego ideal even though he is doing nothing toward achieving it or has he accepted an inadequate self-concept?

Is he hopeful, does he have some optimism in his outlook on life? Is he fighting for gratification even with inappropriate objects for gratification, or has he given up?

If the answers to most of these questions indicate that ego strength, flexibility and struggle still predominate, some negatives will not necessarily interfere with the ultimate prospects for treatment.

Any adolescent who can be led into forming a treatment relationship and who will continue to come for appointments offers some hope. If, in addition, the adolescent's parents are cooperative, the possibilities for a favorable outcome, for some amelioration of the problems increase. Even when the preliminary diagnostic survey leaves the counselor with serious reservations about the prognosis it may be worth while to attempt to engage the adolescent in treatment.

The first meeting with an adolescent should start with a positive statement, perhaps expressing pleasure in the meeting, and should end with a direct expectation that the adolescent is going to return. With some adolescents appropriate physical contact is useful, a pat on the shoulder or a handshake.

Many adolescents respond to being treated like important guests. A tour of the office suite (if there is more than one office) dispels some of the fear of the unknown environment; an introduction to a receptionist or other relevant personnel emphasizes the importance of the adolescent's status. The counselor may express interest in his physical comfort, particularly when temperatures are extreme, or when the adolescent has had to travel a considerable distance. Soft drinks and cookies or candy may be available; an adolescent who arrives directly from school for an appointment is actually hungry. The real feeding has the implicit value of pointing up the gratifying nature of the relationship.

The adolescent is greeted as if he were an adult. The counselor shows respect for his attitudes and values, asks for his opinions and listens carefully to the responses. Adolescents are surprised and flattered at such attention. Most adults talk down to them or talk at them; few listen to what the adolescent says.

Frequently adolescents are opinionated, narcissistic, masking uncertainties by a know-it-all attitude. Their talk is often boring and repetitive, reflecting poor judgment based on erroneous and half-digested information. The dynamic meaning of much of what they say is obvious and offers temptation to the counselor to interpret, but the temptation should be resisted. Any comment which the adolescent senses as critical will make him cling more stubbornly to his own point of view. The chief complaint of most adolescents is that they are not understood. By listening, without interruption and with the serious intention to understand, the counselor shows his genuine interest.

The adolescent will sense the counselor's recognition of his worth. The attention evokes and feeds his narcissism and makes the adolescent feel good. It helps toward the establishment of a positive feeling toward the counselor. In addition, he will be more receptive to the opinion of the adult after he has had full opportunity to express his own point of view and defend it unchallenged.

Where there have been chronic problems the adolescent is given opportunity to spill his resentment about all the adults who have talked to him, usually critically, in earlier attempts to solve his difficulties.

An insightful interpretation, general rather than in depth, easily comprehended and without negative affect, may be given to the adolescent in the first contact and indicates to him that the counselor is capable of understanding him. It allows the adolescent to see that the counselor is trying to understand him in a helpful manner that other adults in his life have not used. Adolescents crave understanding; they will usually react positively to an indication that they are understood. Clear, not too subtle comments indicating recognition of his feelings can help win the adolescent into the beginning relationship and into continued treatment. Such statements as, "You must have been frightened," or, "You must have felt bad about that," go beneath the surface description of an incident, indicate deeper levels of understanding and awareness of affects.

The counselor does not at first challenge the adolescent's defenses. In whatever manner the adolescent states his problems, his statement is listened to without criticism, no attempt is made to find fault, or to correct attitudes and behavior. The counselor places himself temporarily on the side of the adolescent. He empathizes with the adolescent's present emotional situation. Often many other adults in his life have tried to change the adolescent and have been critical of what he says and does. The counselor lets him see that he takes it for granted the adolescent must have had reasons for thinking and acting as he has.

While the counselor may not be able to condone some particular act, he can be sympathetic. He may say, "It is too bad that you felt you had to do thus and so." This implies understanding that there are reasons which impelled the behavior and offers hope that alternate methods of behavior, more gratifying or more acceptable, can be made available.

It is important to let the adolescent save face. He is much concerned with maintaining his pride and integrity which frequently have been damaged by the behavior which precipitated the referral for treatment.

Careful study of the background history, together with the quick intuitive impression as the counselor sees the adolescent for the first time, will help to vary the approach according to the specific needs of a particular adolescent. An over-controlled adolescent may be uncomfortable with informality. For example, the counselor may tilt back his chair to indicate ease and in the hope of minimizing anxiety, but the adolescent with a compulsive character formation may feel this as inefficiency, carelessness or condescension. He can trust only a more structured approach. Or, the hostilely suspicious adolescent may react with anxiety to great warmth. His problems center around his fears of close relationships. His response to warmth may be increased suspicion and even withdrawal. His fears lessen when there is a degree of emotional distance between him and the counselor. A business-like straightforward professional manner will achieve the necessary distance. With some adolescents the counselor will be paternal, maternal or fraternal; some respond to spontaneity, others need an orderly and intellectualized approach.

Adolescents tend to "fall in love" with the counselor to whom they first confess their difficulties. The practice in many social agencies of interviewing an adolescent for diagnostic purposes and then transferring him to another counselor for ongoing treatment has many disadvantages. Adolescents frequently are considered difficult to retain in treatment but some of the difficulties may stem from these transfers. Adolescents are anxious enough about their approach to a treatment setting without the necessity for relating to different counselors initially.

After an adolescent has been in treatment and has established a relationship with his counselor it is possible, when special factors make it necessary or advisable, to effect transfer without causing the adolescent to terminate treatment. Such transfers can be prepared and the separation anxiety can usually be worked through.

In some few specific instances transfer to another counselor may be indicated by individual needs, but in general adolescents should be protected whenever possible from change of counselors.

Some adolescents will be resistive in spite of all efforts. When the adolescent says he does not want a second appointment, he may be asked to "give it a whirl" for a short time. Or the resistance may be interpreted with recognition of underlying anxiety, even if the specific nature of the anxiety is not yet understood. "This is new. It's only natural to feel funny about it." An adolescent who states definitely that he is not going to return can sometimes be induced to accept another appointment by a statement such as, "Come in next week and tell me why you don't think this is going to help."

It is important to communicate that the counselor takes it for granted the adolescent will return. The continuation is implicit in the way the counselor sets up future appointment schedules, in his manner that assumes there will be continuation of contact. The wise counselor does not phrase a question so that it can be answered negatively or positively unless he is prepared to accept either answer. If an adolescent is asked if he wishes to return and replies that he does not, the counselor is placed in the position of arguing him out of a decision already formulated. A positive statement from the counselor such as "see you on Tuesday" leaves the adolescent less room for defensive refusal of needed help.

When an adult starts treatment he is usually motivated to endure whatever pain or anxiety the treatment situation will produce. He hopes he will eventually derive benefit but he can endure waiting and he can continue in treatment even though he does not get immediate satisfaction or quick amelioration of his problems.

An adolescent however ordinarily does not seek treatment for himself; the process is imposed upon him for outside sources and at the beginning he does not participate voluntarily. An adolescent often mistrusts adults and their capacity for understanding him. Almost universally he is anxious about his private mental life; he does not want anyone touching the frightening, defended-against conflictual issues and he fears a counselor may read his mind. Very often he feels his problems are caused by others rather than due to forces within himself and he does not see how treatment for himself will solve his troubles.

There are occasional adolescents who themselves initiate treatment. These are usually introspective, articulate adolescents who send out a cry for help, often by creating a crisis at home or elsewhere. Frequently this occurs by means of material they write, diaries, letters, sometimes even school essays, so frightening in emotional tone or subject matter that the adult response is a quick referral for help. The diaries, ostensibly private, are placed where parents cannot avoid seeing them; letters, unsealed, are left where they are readily found. This type of writing is a plea for a relationship that will be understanding as well as corrective. So, often, are threats of suicide and threatened or actual runaways from home. These adolescents reveal their need more or less directly and are motivated for treatment.

More often, however, the adolescent has been forced into treatment. He does not see it as his own choice of action, or he comes because of the problem areas of his life, where he least expects gratification. He may actually be hungering for a relationship but if his initial anxieties about treatment are ignored, the anxiety may override the wish for the relationship.

The adolescent may be pushed into coming for one appointment, but he will not continue unless, at the outset, his anxiety has been allayed, his fears about the magical (seeing inside him, reading his thoughts) have been quieted, and a positive interaction between him and the counselor has conveyed hopefulness. It is the initial task of the counselor to make the experience sufficiently gratifying and to meet some immediate needs quickly enough to insure that the adolescent will return. It is important from the beginning to look for ways to be directly helpful, to lessen environmental pressures or give advice. The counselor can ask how he can help and the concrete offer cements the adolescent's hope that he can count on the counselor.

When the counselor understands that his first contacts with an adolescent are directed to winning over, his own anxiety about correct treatment techniques is relieved, his emphasis shifts from consideration of steps in treatment to building the relationship. Then, his own creativity, his human reactions to the adolescent, will lead to appropriate responses to specific adolescents.

The first interviews are used to build a relationship by a common-sense approach based on sensitivity to adolescent needs. No attempt is made to interpret in depth. Any insights that are used are in the language and at the level that are immediately understandable to the adolescent. A counselor who considers that treatment consists exclusively of acquiring insight into un-

conscious processes and who concentrates only on the underlying meaning of what is said, may convey to the adolescent a
feeling of being detached, distant, and lacking in genuine concern. Additionally, a premature attempt to give insight will
frighten the adolescent.

The counselor communicates his wish to be helpful, his
interest in the adolescent and his hope for the resolution of
problems. He bases his approach on the universal longings for
meaningful and gratifying relations. His voice, manner and his
words hold out implicit hope that the adolescent and he together
can build such a relationship.

Everyone feels the affective tone of certain places or people;
hostility, warmth, or friendliness all communicate themselves.
Characteristically, adolescents are much more sensitive to affective atmosphere than adults because they are not so consistently
defended. They perceive, often without being able to verbalize,
the affective tone of various relationships and react to the feelings they sense rather than to the words that are spoken. The
counselor must remember that the adolescent will react to extremely subtle nuances of affect. A counselor may say the right
thing to an adolescent without the anticipated result if the adolescent senses that the counselor's affect is different from his words.

The counselor must be active during the early interviews. He
must be the one who does the giving; he cannot expect an
adolescent to be able to give, in words or feelings. The adolescent should not be kept guessing about how much the counselor
knows about him and his problems. Ideally, the adolescent
should be able to state his problems and his understanding of
why he was referred for treatment. But if he cannot, or does
not wish to, the counselor helps him. The counselor can tell him
how his parents, or his school or others, have stated the difficulties and asks for the adolescent's own point of view. The
adolescent will know then that the counselor has not totally
accepted the problems as defined by others, but also places importance on the adolescent's opinion. Tension is relieved by

getting the complaints others have made about him out into the open. The air is cleared with a nonjudgmental statement of the main problems, as others see them and as the adolescent sees his own situation.

This procedure also counteracts the adolescent's tendency to restrict the problem areas or to avoid them. It reduces his fantasies about what the counselor knows about him. Openness and fairness in asking for his own viewpoint usually appeal to the adolescent and help to build trust and confidence. The way in which he responds serves to add to the counselor's diagnostic appraisal. His discussion of his own problems gives clues to the nature of his defenses, his anxiety, his ability to see his own involvement in his difficulties and some information about his attitudes towards significant people in his life.

Unasked-for advice and active direction is avoided because adolescents generally feel that adults maneuver them and tell them how to live their lives. Actually adolescents do not have enough experience for complete independence, and although they may resent it, they are indeed dependent on adults. An offer of intervention is more acceptable, however, if it comes from someone the adolescent feels has previously treated him like an adequate independent human being. While treating him with the respect that would be given to an adult, the counselor keeps in mind that the adolescent is not totally capable of making mature judgments or responsible adult decisions. If the counselor is called on, early in the contact, to intervene actively on behalf of the adolescent (with courts, schools, or even with parents) he should first engage the cooperation of the adolescent, offer his suggestions and be prepared to discuss them and alternatives with the adolescent.

It is not necessary in the beginning that an adolescent admit his need for treatment in so many words; it is more important for him to wish to return. The counselor will know, without any verbalizations, when the relationship has assumed meaning for the adolescent. Verbalization of motivation is sometimes confused with actual motivation. It is important for the adolescent to be motivated for treatment but it is not essential for that motivation to be put into words. Too often resistance, which is to be expected in an adolescent, is confused with lack of motivation. If an adolescent continues to keep appointments, the counselor may be certain that he is motivated for treatment.

In the initial process of discussing the problems and how the adolescent views them, the counselor's aim is to reach a tacit agreement about the focus of treatment. The partnership is emphasized; nothing will be done *to* the adolescent; he and the counselor will work together to understand the difficulties and to make life less painful for the adolescent.

The steps by which the adolescent is motivated toward setting mutual goals for ongoing treatment consist of:

building a positive relationship,
siding with the adolescent in issues between him and others,
showing interest in whatever interests him,
being giving and reassuring,
encouraging hope for alleviation of problems and fulfillment
  of longings.

The counselor should be prepared for direct questions which may deal with serious issues. The adolescent may ask questions about the nature of the treatment and its outcome. These are important and must not be dismissed by the counselor. The questions cannot be answered as though to another professional or only on the basis of theory and clinical findings. A response on a pedantic or clinical level will drive the adolescent away. An adult in treatment may be told that the counselor does not know what the outcome will be. An adolescent wants hope for gratification spelled out to him immediately or he will not return. For example, the counselor may say, "I have helped others with troubles like yours," and hope is implicit both in the statement and in his tone of voice and manner.

The counselor must always remember the hopefulness of the adolescent and his relative inability to accept unfulfillment. If he wants to keep the adolescent in treatment, his answers to questions about prognosis and procedures must carry a hopeful note. Since there are few adolescents who will not gain at least minimal benefits from treatment, the gravity of the diagnosis, in the counselor's opinion, need not diminish the communication of hope to the adolescent.

Many adolescents will ask directly, "What's the matter with me?" or "Why is everybody down on me?" But few adolescents are interested in hearing a clinical name for the disorder. The adolescent wants to know the cause of his emotional turmoil and how he can be helped to feel better or happier. His questions should be answered along these same lines. For example, an adolescent says he feels miserable and wants to know, "Why is everybody else better than me?" He can be told, "Your feelings now have to do with feelings you've had earlier in your life about other people, maybe about the people in your immediate family. If we can get to understand how these feelings came about, you will feel much better about yourself."

An obese adolescent girl may ask immediately, "Can you make me thin?" The answer must be phrased in a way that generates hope without giving a guarantee in time or pounds. The response will be based on the counselor's knowledge that people who overeat are searching for gratifications. The obese girl can be told, "We will find out what's going on to make you overweight and then we can see what can be done about it." This answer shifts the emphasis from diet to other unfulfilled longings.

The adolescent has the right, just as an adult does, to inquire about the counselor's professional qualifications and training. Personal questions are more likely to be asked after the relationship is firmly established and their meaning will be clear to the counselor from the context in which they occur. When the questions are inappropriately personal, the adolescent will know they will not be answered even as he asks and will not resent it if the counselor responds with, "Why do you ask that?" Or, even better, "That may be an important question. Let's find out more about why you asked."

The questions asked early in the relationship always need to be seen as a testing of the counselor. The adolescent is in effect asking, "Are you just like all the others, or are you really going to help me?"

Adolescents frequently do not want to acknowledge that they have problems; they do not see themselves as playing a part in their troubles; they tend to project on to others. They feel all their difficulties will be solved if others change. In the process of engagement in treatment this stance needs to be corrected to the position of a therapeutic alliance in which the adolescent and his counselor work together on the problems. The problems constitute a kind of jigsaw puzzle in which both are interested and on which they will work cooperatively to put the pieces together. When this point is reached, the beginning phase, the process of engaging the adolescent into treatment is completed, and the helping process can move on.

# 7

# General Considerations
# in Treatment

IN THE FIRST contacts with an adolescent the counselor works to create a situation in which the adolescent looks upon the counselor as a child views his parents, that is, as the source of gratification. Once the counselor has established this kind of relationship he is in a position to teach, in the profound sense, a better way of functioning. Out of love from the parents the young child incorporates parental attitudes, accepting that the parental way is the right way of functioning for himself. Ideally, what he has learned from his parents is an acceptable manner of functioning which allows him to go on in life with a minimum of inner difficulty. What the counselor deals with in treatment are the conflicts, the distortions or negative expectations from life which the adolescent brings with him which interfere with his normal personality growth and which result in behavior that creates suffering and difficulties. Treatment consists of an alteration process.

In the context of a sustained positive relationship the counselor attempts to make it possible for the adolescent to present his past and present conflicts and fears and to deal with them. The adolescent senses the affective tone of the relationship and the counselor's genuine concern for him, and within that emotional atmosphere, the counselor helps to correct the deficits in the adolescent's functioning. Then the adolescent can test some of the attitudes and feelings about which he has conflict.

During the initial process of winning the adolescent over into a therapeutic alliance, goals have been formulated. It is important that counselor and adolescent have the same goals and that the adolescent should know how he and the counselor intend to work. This mutual understanding helps keep the course of treatment directed toward the major issues. But even if the adolescent wanders the counselor constantly keeps the goals in mind and keeps the treatment moving in the direction indicated by the ultimate aims.

Some counselors fear the dependent relationship that grows between themselves and an adolescent. Recognizing that adolescence is the time for developing independence the counselor may become anxious over the extent of the dependent tie. But it is only within a dependency relationship that an adolescent can be helped to grow up. Allowing dependency longings to be expressed in the relationship is a healthy experience, promoting maturation. The adolescent who has had unfulfilled dependency wishes learns that some gratification is possible and can regain hope that he can ultimately find satisfactory relationship on a more adult and independent level. The treatment process with many adolescents is one of feeding, sometimes literally, of nurturing, fostering, fathering and mothering.

Some adolescent boys with strong masculine strivings may deny their dependent needs because they equate them with femininity. These boys profit from a relationship with a male counselor who is understanding, warm and sensitive, to correct the mistaken notion that these qualities are exclusively feminine. With such a counselor the adolescent can become more tolerant of his own dependency needs and the pseudo-masculinity, which is defensive against a feared femininity, is also corrected.

Out of this dependency adolescents frequently want to establish a personal relationship with the counselor. It is not un-common for an unhappy adolescent to ask if he may come to live with his counselor. The request often indicates the adolescent's hunger for closeness and is answered in relation to the problem the adolescent is actually trying to solve. "I know things are tough at home now, but some day you'll find they're better." Attempts to pursue personal contacts may also indicate curiosity and testing; if they are handled casually by the counselor, the adolescent usually does not persist.

Almost inevitably the adolescent will ask questions about the personal life of the counselor, different in focus and intent from the questioning at the beginnings of contact. The counselor must always ask himself why the questions were asked. Sometimes a straightforward answer fills a real need for the adolescent. Questions about education or marital status may be a search for establishing an ego ideal. Other, more personal questions need not be answered, but the counselor must always acknowledge the legitimacy of the curiosity.

All such personal matters can be handled without anxiety if limits have already been set and clearly defined in a benign non-judgmental way. It is ordinary professional practice to set limits on any therapeutic relationship but with adolescents it is essential. Usually this can be accomplished by tacit communication of attitudes about what is allowed and what is not permitted. The type of relationship which develops is based on the counselor's understanding of the individual adolescent and his needs. Defining the limits within that relationship is valuable not only for the adolescent but also for the counselor. The understanding of limits avoids resentment and other negative countertransference reactions on the part of the counselor. Provocative or testing behavior may irritate the counselor or make him anxious. To set limits at that point, with irritation, will cause the adolescent to feel rebuffed or rejected. The hostility or annoyance is the counselor's problem, not the adolescent's.

In treatment with adults the sessions are generally serious;

the adult usually does not want to waste time and he is motivated to work steadily on his problems. With adolescents, the situation may be different. An adolescent will not be eager to return if every hour is soul-searching and painful. The counselor attempts to create and develop a light touch; some degree of lightness lessens the anxiety around the issues. He indicates both by words and manner that the problems are not as serious, as unique, as earth-shaking, as the adolescent fears. Some adolescents take matters so gravely that a light comment from the counselor is indicated to give perspective and relieve anxiety. The counselor's mood and approach should counterbalance the intensity of the adolescent's.

Adolescents tend to recite their current activities of the day or week and some may chatter almost aimlessly about what has occurred since the previous interview. The counselor will listen, but it may be necessary for him to break into such a recital with a comment that directs the adolescent toward the therapeutic goal. For example, "Why do you think this happened?" or "What do you think about this incident?" Such comments serve two purposes. First, attention is directed to the fact that there is something to be gained from looking for the answer, from searching for causes and effects, for reactions to the people in the adolescent's life, and for the part he himself played in bringing about whatever he is describing. Secondly, it alerts the adolescent to his own participation in the therapeutic exploration. The counselor does not at first tell him why something happened. Instead, he asks the adolescent how he reacted in the situation and how he feels about the occurrence. The counselor may then add an additional possible explanation.

The counselor sometimes allows the adolescent to talk even if what he says appears to be without real meaning, limited to detailed descriptions of incidents or the plots of movies. He does not interrupt to bring up controversial, negative or charged issues, although he may interject comments indicating interest and understanding, directed at meaningful interpretation of what is being said. If this kind of communication continues over a long period of time the counselor must determine from his own understanding of the adolescent's character structure whether the chatter is only resistance. Sometimes the talk may be important for the adolescent as a means of getting full undivided attention; it may be a cover for what is going on internally; or it may be an indirect method of communicating what the adolescent is fearful of saying directly.

Frequently adolescents begin treatment with undirected or playful talk but later become seriously involved in dealing with the important emotional issues of their lives. The skill of the counselor will make it possible for him to know when the adolescent is ready to move into and deal more directly with underlying issues.

A special problem arises with the noncommunicative nonverbal adolescent who says very little and does not discuss meaningful material. In such instances it is difficult to assess what goes on at a nonverbal level of communication. The adolescent may come to feel loved and valued, grow to feel more masculine or more feminine through the relationship which may be in and of itself a gratifying growth experience. Through this process of being nourished changes may occur, even though within the therapeutic sessions communication is minimal or remains on the level of friendly exchange. It is especially important in these situations to maintain communication with the parents who can describe actual changes in behavior and attitudes in the functioning of the adolescent.

One girl whose chief interest was in horseback riding and whose life centered around the stables remained in treatment for two years with a motherly warm counselor. She talked almost exclusively about horses, brought pictures of horses as gifts to decorate the office walls. But during this time the girl became softer and more feminine; her relationships with the boys she knew as riding companions changed as she shifted her role from "one of the boys" to a boy-girl relationship. There are many young boys who talk endlessly about automobiles and, recently, sessions are often devoted to space rockets.

The counselor's language is important and speech should be adapted to the adolescent's level of comprehension. Pedantic or academic terminology will seem patronizing to many adolescents, creating distance between them and the counselor, although occasionally an adolescent will feel his intelligence is being acknowledged by the use of scientific terms or multisyllabic words. An adolescent is usually pleased if he is asked for the exact meaning of his current slang or the in-group words that he uses, especially if the counselor subsequently makes occasional use of the words to indicate that he has accepted them.

The adolescent who gropes for words to describe parts of the body or body functions or sexual behavior may not know the correct terms or may know only street language. Adolescent girls are less likely than boys to know street terms; in many instances they are amazingly ignorant of any terminology, acceptable or unacceptable, and may have to be educated to a vocabulary for body parts and functioning.

It is helpful if the counselor suggests proper terminology in a casual and unstilted manner in order to clarify meaning. Upon occasion, defensiveness may be broken through by the counselor's use of the adolescent's own vocabulary, perhaps with a joking reference to the fact that the adolescent uses different words with his friends than he does with the counselor. When there is frequent use of street language or profanity for shock purposes or out of habit or because the adolescent has a limited vocabulary, the counselor will discourage this practice and will himself use correct terms.

Physical activity during a therapeutic session is fairly frequent with young adolescents. They swing arms and legs, fiddle with objects on the desk, even walk around the room. Many of these movements are simply tension-relieving mechanisms. The counselor would not interfere unless they make communication impossible. Often the movements are unconsciously masturbatory and these are not interfered with or interpreted unless the adolescent himself brings it up out of his own concern. Most adolescents are concerned about masturbation but they rarely talk about it. When they do, the counselor need only reassure and understand.

Adolescents are often reluctant to ask directly for help, even though they may be relieved if the counselor offers to help extricate them from a difficult situation which they are not able to handle appropriately. An adolescent who says he is going to run away from home may be persuaded to postpone action. The counselor expresses understanding of the feelings that prompt the desire to run away and suggests an immediate appointment to talk further about plans and reasons. In the same way an adolescent who contemplates dropping out of school may be told, "Come in to see me and let's talk about your decision."

Often adolescents can be deterred from precipitous action if the counselor volunteers to be immediately available. Habitual truanting or cutting classes may be curbed if the counselor says, "The next time you feel you have to cut out, call me up and we'll talk about it." A willingness to answer the phone sympathetically at seven in the morning may keep an adolescent in high school.

Adolescents tend to magnify the critical nature of some situations and discussion helps to clarify the problem for both the counselor and the adolescent. A high school student says he hates his math teacher and will no longer attend the class. The counselor does not immediately offer to arrange for a change in the school situation even where it may be possible to do so. He suggests instead that the adolescent talk more about the particular teacher. The discussion may indicate what specifically the adolescent is reacting to in the teacher and whether the distaste for the class arises out of the personality of the teacher or of the adolescent.

Adolescents may complicate difficulties because pride and

stubbornness sometimes interfere with their own ability to retract, yield or compromise. These situations gain from full discussion before the counselor offers advice or intervention, when there is time. But adolescent problems often erupt into crisis situations and the counselor may have to take action immediately to prevent serious consequences.

There may also be occasions when the counselor must take action that the adolescent does not want him to take but which may nevertheless be in the best interest of the adolescent. Confidences about illegitimate pregnancies or projected elopements or runaways from home may have to be shared with the parents. Preferably, the adolescent can be helped to tell his parents himself, but if he cannot or will not, the counselor must act. The adolescent is a minor and his parents retain responsibility for him, legally and morally. The adolescent should always be told what is going to be done and why; if the relationship is strong enough this need not interfere with the future course of treatment.

Some adolescents tend to depreciate their counselor. They are chiefly over-compensated or acting-out adolescents. No one enjoys being depreciated and this attitude may arouse negative feelings in the counselor. But the situation is more easily tolerated if he recognizes that the need to depreciate is part of the adolescent's character structure.

These adolescents will tell the counselor that he is not hip; that he is not with it. When a clue is obtained about the specific reasons why the adolescent needs to belittle his counselor, the reasons should be interpreted to the adolescent, provided that he is already involved in a continuing relationship. The counselor will focus on why it is important for the adolescent to feel that he knows better than the counselor. If, for example, the evidence shows that one parent depreciates the other, the counselor will tell the adolescent that he feels about his counselor the way his mother feels about his father. He would then go on to point out to the adolescent why he needs to feel this way. "You feel better about yourself if you ride me the way your mother does your father."

Interpretations are important because if the adolescent continues the depreciation it interferes with his ability to identify with the counselor. Furthermore, depreciation interferes with the adolescent's conscious recognition that the treatment has serious significance.

Direct interpretations of unconscious material are unacceptable in the treatment of adolescents. The adolescent defends himself strenuously even against conscious unacceptable thoughts and feelings; much more strongly does he maintain his defenses against the frightening unconscious. Interpretation without adequate preparation will seem bizarre and ludicrous to the adolescent. The counselor himself must always be aware of the unconscious forces. However he speaks to the adolescent on a conscious common-sense level about issues of which the adolescent can be aware.

Oedipal material is especially frightening to adolescents. It must be dealt with cautiously and patiently; and adolescents cannot be pushed into discussion of, or insight into, oedipal conflicts. Many adolescents have conscious oedipal fantasies which they quickly repress out of anxiety. Some universalization of this experience through a carefully timed comment will help alleviate anxiety. Adolescents will talk quite freely about the competitive aspects of the parental relationship. A boy will say without anxiety that his father thinks he knows it all, or a girl complain that her mother is old-fashioned in her ideas about cosmetics or dress. But the sexual interest or involvement with parents is forbidden and therefore repressed; it is too disturbing to be dealt with directly. Older adolescents, approaching adulthood, who have been in treatment over a period of time, come to more direct discussion and acceptance of oedipal interpretations but the process is a slow one.

The counselor should not be seduced by the eager adolescent, usually intelligent and sophisticated, who demands insight immediately. The demand is a wish for closeness or for something more basic in the relationship with the counselor and should be recognized as such. Sometimes an adolescent who has read psychological material thinks his counselor will not otherwise be interested in him and he is prepared to pay the price for the sake of the relationship.

While adolescents are not pushed toward insight, the counselor orients them toward attempts to control and correct their behavior and conveys the idea that understanding the causes will be helpful to them in doing so. This is done by comments such as, "How do you explain this trouble you got into?" or "Why do you suppose you did that?" In the long run the adolescent will move toward self-understanding, and hopefully, when the adolescent ego is more mature, he will be able to gain deeper insight into his unconscious motivations.

Adolescents do not ordinarily bring dream material into treatment. If an adolescent does report dreams, the counselor will use the material for himself to gain insight into what is going on within the adolescent but without direct interpretation and without making his interest so obvious or absorbing that the adolescent may then make an effort to please by becoming preoccupied with reporting dreams or with dream interpretation. The counselor can casually ask what the adolescent thinks his dream means. The information and any associations that spontaneously occur are used for the counselor's greater understanding of the problems.

For example, an adolescent boy reported a dream which clearly indicated castration anxiety and fear of girls. No direct interpretation of the dream was given but at an appropriate moment the counselor asked this boy why he should expect to be hurt if he asked a girl for a date. If after reporting such a dream the adolescent persisted in further discussion of the dream itself, a common-sense question, such as, "Do you have to be afraid of girls?" would alleviate the anxiety around sex which the dream expressed, and further cement the adolescent's feeling that the counselor understood and accepted him.

In adult treatment the purpose of dream interpretation is to loosen defenses as well as to develop insight. Adolescence is a period in which constructive defenses are necessary. The adolescent ego is not ready to handle preconscious and unconscious material directly. Adolescents do not want to reveal their own unconscious, partly out of anxiety over what others will think. In any case, a direct interpretation of dream material usually promotes resistance in an adolescent. He will feel that the counselor is reading his mind which is anxiety-provoking and the adolescent will need to depreciate the interpretation. The counselor will be more successful with indirect handling of whatever intrapsychic conflicts the dreams reveal.

The counselor does not try to undo adolescent defenses unless they are creating difficulties in the environment or within the individual. If some specific defense must be altered in order to effect a treatment goal, an attempt is made to do so. For example, a sixteen-year-old boy says that he does not consider dating important and that there are better things in life to think about than girls or sex. He is not going to give up his high principles to attain a better social life. These expressed attitudes are the outcome of a complex of defenses. They are ego syntonic, give him a sense of superiority and a feeling that he is "good." But his attitudes are obviously inappropriate for a boy his age and are defensive against sexuality and sexual impulses. Ordinarily, time itself would alter the structure of these defenses, but if the boy is exceedingly uncomfortable about his social situation, then, within the context of a secure relationship, the counselor may help the boy understand his fears about sexuality.

Any attempt to alter the defensive posture too early results in frightening the adolescent or in re-enforcing his defenses. The counselor goes along with the defenses in the beginning in the service of cementing the relationship. After the relationship is secure, the process becomes one of gradual alteration through confrontation, reorientation, and suggestions about alternatives. As a general consideration no defense should be attacked directly early in treatment.

Some categories of defenses ought not be undone in adolescents. Any defenses that are being used against depressed feelings should be left untouched. The depressed adolescent is in any case difficult to treat. Whatever defenses he is using to bolster his feelings of being lovable or worthwhile should be supported. Even if the defenses against depression take the form of self-aggrandizement, boasting, self-reassurances and fantasies of success, they should not be undone. The basically depressed adolescent who has acquired some illusory defenses such as a fantasy of popularity should not be interfered with for fear that the underlying depression will be precipitated. The adolescent will eventually offer an opportunity to the counselor for modifying these distortions.

Defenses against depression or feelings of worthlessness cannot be shifted without offering alternatives. The adolescent does not have the resources that are available to an adult for gratification. Because the adolescent response to the counselor is childlike, re-creating the original parent-child relationship, the counselor offers himself as a resource for gratification and this gratification becomes an alternative for the adolescent which may make it possible in time for him to yield his defenses. The adolescent who feels worthless and who depreciates himself needs to have his defenses bolstered by his counselor. Wholesome sublimatory defenses are always encouraged under these circumstances.

When the basic needs of any individual have not been met in early life that individual develops defenses against such needs. "I don't need anybody." "Who needs love?" If the early deprivations were profound, it is sometimes impossible ever to compensate; individuals with no experience of receiving cannot be given to readily. While the question may be raised theoretically whether or not basic lacks can ever be provided in treatment, with adolescents the effort must be made. Adolescents can learn new devices to cover up their basic deficiencies so that later in life the defensive techniques may provide an adequate enough resolution.

Frequently adolescents start treatment with defenses shaken because of some recently experienced crisis or failure. Treatment will be aimed toward correction by encouraging good defenses, by teaching other modes of behavior and by providing a relationship and the resources for gaining other relationships.

What is being defended against dictates the timing of attempts to alter defenses. Too quickly loosening the neurotic defense of inhibition in an adolescent girl may result in sexual promiscuity. Whether the counselor presses toward alteration of any defense or moves slowly depends on special circumstances in the environment as well as within the individual.

In the course of treatment individual factors determine how to deal with the defenses. The counselor must always consider the purpose of the defense, the adequacy of the personality structure of the adolescent, the timing in treatment, environmental factors and the availability of alternative sources of gratification.

Many adolescents have conflict over hostile impulses. The counselor helps the adolescent in two important aspects of hostility conflict. The adolescent may be afraid of his hostility and defend against recognizing and feeling the hostility. Or the adolescent may be angry without knowing why his hostility is aroused. The counselor encourages the appropriate expression of hostile feelings in words, rather than action. He helps the adolescent to give up the defenses against feeling. But it is equally important to help the adolescent learn the causes especially if the hostility is aroused by infantile and irrational reasons. If the hostility is inappropriate or acted on excessively or destructively, understanding of the origin of the hostility helps in learning better controls.

Within the therapeutic relationship the adolescent is given

permission to express his feelings. When an adolescent discovers that he can express hostility without destroying his counselor or losing his affection or without changing the essential nature of the relationship, he has undergone a corrective emotional experience. He may find that he can feel anger toward the counselor and even express his anger openly; the counselor remains concerned with the adolescent and is neither frightened nor discouraged by the adolescent's anger but instead helps him to discover whatever motivational or infantile causes may be involved. The adolescent discovers that his hostile feelings are not as damaging nor as unique as he previously thought and he further learns that he does not need to defend himself against the affect of hostility in the pathological manner he has been using.

The usual procedure is for the adolescent to come once a week for an hour session. However, during the course of treatment for some adolescents more frequent interviews may be necessary and the counselor should always be flexible about the appointment schedule. In many situations it is helpful for the adolescent to be told his counselor will be available at any critical time for phone conversations or additional interviews.

The technique of ending the session is sometimes a problem with adolescents. Because the dependent relationship is carefully fostered by the counselor the adolescent is often reluctant to leave. It is not advisable early in the relationship to interpret the need to cling; it is important for the adolescent to feel the need for closeness with his counselor because this is the basic tool of the helping process. Walking the adolescent to the door with a casual "See you next time," sometimes serves to terminate the session; with other adolescents the clinging may be dealt with directly but without creating feelings of rejection. A comment such as, "I know you hate to leave, but I'll see you next week," touches on the underlying issue without debasing or denying the need. The adolescent who has the final appointment of the day may want to remain while the counselor clears his desk. He should be allowed to do so and he can be asked to turn off the light, close the door, or perform some similar small act which signifies closing. In this way the adolescent is eased out without making an issue about the clinging or creating undue anxiety about it.

In contrast are those adolescents who wish to leave early. Again, in general, the basic issues would not be taken up directly at first. Such questions as "What's the rush?" or "Why are you so antsy today?" deal with the matter lightly while leaving an opening for further discussion if the adolescent is ready and willing to talk. Sometimes an intermission, such as going out for a soft drink, may cut through the tensions. But if the adolescent is so anxious that he cannot endure the interview he should be given permission to leave when he chooses. This is less anxiety-provoking than a painful clock-watching session. Later in treatment the counselor would investigate to determine whether the wish to leave early comes out of anxiety about feelings aroused within that particular session.

Adolescents cannot be treated if the counselor insists on the rigid application of any one theoretical or technical approach. No matter what his own orientation, the counselor must be flexible and prepared to relate the treatment to the needs of the adolescent. Some who will not accept one-to-one treatment may be willing to attend group treatment. Others can be helped indirectly by working with their parents and/or teachers; when the environmental pressures are alleviated the negative adolescent behavior will frequently improve.

But if the treatment goal is some alleviation of inner conflict and modification of habitual ways of responding, the adolescent must be engaged directly in the helping process.

The prime consideration is that the adolescent keep appointments since obviously it is impossible to help him if he is not there. It is not essential in the beginning that he desire help. The counselor must be patient and ingenious in finding ways to win over the adolescent and establish a meaningful relationship.

While an adolescent may come initially because he is being forced or threatened by parents, school, court and others, it is virtually impossible for anyone to make him continue to do something he does not wish to do. Thus, an adolescent who continues to come, even if he is seemingly unresponsive, full of reservations and doubts, is finding something of value in the treatment.

# 8

# Special Considerations in Treatment

CERTAIN KINDS of adolescent behavior are so pervasive or so flagrant that the counselor's attention may become fixed on the symptoms. The immediate impact of hostility or stubbornness, blandness or brashness may be so great that it interferes with the ordinary helping approach to the adolescent.

These adolescents may be difficult to engage in treatment in any case. But if the counselor relates to the symptomatic behavior, treatment becomes almost impossible. The adults in the life of the adolescent, even those who have wanted to help him, have usually been reacting to his behavior. The counselor, if he is to be effective, must not fall into the trap of addressing the surface. He must be able, quickly, to give the adolescent a response and a kind of understanding he has not met with from others. The counselor must touch some chord that lets the adolescent feel he is finding a new and more meaningful relationship that offers hope of gratification. Fuller understanding of the characteristic defensive purposes of the behavior helps the counselor to see beneath the surface the adolescent presents to the underlying conflicts.

## The Adolescent Who Denies Difficulties

Many adolescents who are referred for treatment deny that they have any problems although obvious difficulties exist at home, at school, in the community or in peer relationships.

Almost all adolescents show anxiety and some reluctance in the first contact with the counselor and may deny any need for treatment. However, with some reassurance and the correct engaging techniques the majority will soon begin to talk about the troubles that have brought them into treatment.

There are some adolescents from various diagnostic categories who stubbornly assert that they do not have any problems, they see no need for treatment and they may even deny the existence of the difficulties for which they were referred.

Engaging the defensively denying adolescent presents problems because he refuses to admit that he has weaknesses, inhibitions or needs. Initially he presents this defensive aspect of his personality. He may deny that anything at all is wrong in his environment or with him, that he has problems or that he needs treatment. He must remain adequate in the façade he presents. Obviously the counselor cannot immediately undo the defense. But since he recognizes that the adolescent really is fearful, the relationship is first built on the need for closeness to someone who can accept him no matter what he really is.

The adolescent is allowed to discuss whatever he wants to talk about without challenge. The counselor conveys his interest, his desire to help. This is less difficult with the benign overcompensated adolescent than with one who is suspicious, antisocial or paranoid. All of them are defensive over many of the same basic issues, but the overcompensated adolescent is on the whole better organized, not as distrustful and more open to influence by the counselor in spite of his denials.

In addition to establishing the relationship, the counselor has the special task of dealing with the defenses. If they are not dealt with or if they are bolstered by being allowed to go on totally unchallenged, treatment cannot be helpful because the real anxieties are underneath these defenses.

Techniques can be found which will in subtle manner confront the adolescent with his denying mechanisms. This calls for tact and creativity in treatment style. Direct attack upon the denial itself is unacceptable because it carries a negative tone and arouses anxiety. Defensive façades exist because they are necessary to the individual and undermining by the counselor would only serve to create further defensiveness. Comments such as, "Aren't there some things that do bother you?" or "Don't you get worried about yourself once in a while?" may bypass the defensive denial while communicating concern and understanding.

Adolescents who have been forced into treatment by parents or other authorities and whose problems stem from rebellion against authority, often refuse to co-operate out of their rebelliousness. When the adolescent denies problems as an expression of hostile rebelliousness against his parents, other adults, or the established social order, the counselor uses active techniques in the very beginning to engage the adolescent, in spite of his denials. The counselor indicates his recognition of the adolescent's need for denial. Without any trace of accusation the counselor tells him he understands his rebellion is an expression of his anger toward those who have hurt him. The counselor also tells him in which areas of his personality and of his life he must be suffering and how he would benefit from treatment.

No matter how skillfully the counselor approaches him, it may be impossible to get the adolescent to admit that he has difficulties or to get him to return willingly for treatment. Sometimes neither the therapeutic techniques, nor the force of school, legal or parental authority is sufficient to persuade the adolescent into treatment. These are frequently delinquent adolescents whose behavior involves them in serious difficulties in the community. In some instances, if the individual diagnosis warrants it, and all other techniques have failed, these hostile rebellious adolescents may have to be hospitalized in order to initiate treatment, to establish a relationship from which out-patient treatment can later proceed.

When hospitalization is not possible, treatment may be limited to counseling with the parents until such time as further difficulties in the life of the adolescent may lead him to want help.

The counselor must remember that his initial encounter with an adolescent who refuses treatment may create the positive impression that will be decisive at a later date in influencing the adolescent to seek help.

Even if the adolescent continues for many sessions to deny any difficulties the counselor always encourages him to return in the hope that an opportunity will occur in which the adolescent will finally come to admitting some problem. Any admission can then become the starting point for a therapeutic exchange.


## THE ACTING-OUT ADOLESCENT

Adolescents have a tendency to put their impulses into action and to act to resolve their conflicts. The actions may range from the mischievous pranks commonly accepted by the community as due to youthful high spirits to the chronic characteriological actions with serious social and legal consequences. When the actions take the form which leads the adolescent and the community into difficulties they are officially designated as sociopathic, antisocial, delinquent or psychopathic behavior.

The great majority of juvenile delinquents do not become adult criminals. The behavior stops when they become adults. The tendency to act on impulse, the transient rebellions against the superego, and peer group pressures, probably account for the delinquent phase in adolescence.

The major issue in the diagnosis of delinquency is the presence or absence of superego. An adolescent with a good superego may give in temporarily to pressure from his peers to commit antisocial acts, or he may act impulsively, but he comes to realize that delinquency is not a satisfactory adjustment for him. If, however, there is a superego deficiency in adolescence, he may become an adult with a defective superego. In assessing the superego development of the delinquent adolescent, evaluation of the nature of the parental character structures is important. If the parents have adequate superegos the delinquent adolescent is less apt to develop into an adult criminal.

In the adult world some ethical equivocations are prevalent and generally accepted as standard practice by adults who consider themselves honest citizens. Some types of quasi-legal maneuverings, sharp operations and deals, even tax evasions are displayed as evidence of being practical, politic, or clever, not delinquent. Adolescents cannot escape being affected by these cultural superego defects. A father who boasts at the family dinner table about padding his expense accounts or fixing a parking ticket is corrupting his adolescent child's superego.

Certain defenses commonly used by adult criminals appear in adolescent delinquents. Both use projection as a characteristic defense but in an adolescent the projection is more modifiable by treatment. Manipulation is another common defense, not as frequently used by adolescents as by adults. An adult criminal will protest his innocence, put on a show of remorse or adopt other courses designed to influence others or mitigate punishment. Stubbornness and infantile insistence on having his own way is another defense of delinquents. The criminal adult will sometimes yield when it is in his own best interests. But an adolescent will frequently disadvantage himself rather than change his stand.

The attitude of the adolescent toward his own delinquent acts frequently influences the reactions of others in his environment. Sometimes the adolescent's unwillingness to compromise even to a slight degree creates further difficulties for him. A well-timed apology may smooth over school troubles, and an appealing, frightened, seemingly regretful adolescent culprit gets a different reaction from the judge in a court than the swaggering tough who shows no remorse.

Delinquents are difficult to treat and the knowledge of this tends to create a feeling of hopelessness in counselors. But the counselor's feelings contribute to the atmosphere of treatment and treatment does not proceed if both the adolescent and the counselor are discouraged. Any counselor who wishes to treat delinquents must concentrate on evolving techniques for persuading the delinquent adolescent to enter into a relationship instead of focusing on the actual delinquent acts.

In order to be able to work effectively with a delinquent, the counselor must either have a special interest in the problem or must find something in the personality of the individual to which he is sympathetically drawn. Without positive feeling, treatment is not possible, especially with delinquents. Ordinarily it is not desirable to transfer an adolescent from one counselor to another, but if the counselor cannot overcome negative countertransference, he should recognize his own inability to treat this particular adolescent and arrange for another counselor.

Often persons in the environment of the acting-out delinquent become anxious about the behavior and the counselor must be prepared to intercede actively in order to reduce environmental pressures. The counselor must guard against the dangers of over-identifying with the delinquent, becoming angry with people in the environment and perhaps antagonizing them, or, on the other hand, yielding to the pressures too easily, over-emphasizing the environmental concerns and their effects. It is a frequent but oversimplified attitude that holds that an adolescent is untreatable in the community and should be committed to an institution. Counselors occasionally find themselves agreeing to such an easy solution and then rationalize their agreement by exaggerating the difficulties of treatment or the actual extent of the environmental pressures.

The idea of being helped is strange to the delinquent, acting-out adolescent. He may have become accustomed to having adults treat him with suspicion or hostility. He is distrustful and inclined to think that treatment is a trick, designed to entrap him in some way. He may accuse the counselor of using devices or techniques to try to influence him. Although it is true that the counselor uses techniques, these do not negate his interest in helping. The adolescent may ask suspiciously, and from a variety of motives, questions such as, "What's it to you what I do?" "What am I to you?" "What's your racket?" The counselor has to answer simply, honestly and sympathetically that he recognizes the adolescent is unhappy, has difficulties and he wants to help him.

The questioning may imply a wish to be cared for or liked, the desire to be gratified, understood, helped toward integration, or shown a better way of functioning. At the beginning the questions probably relate to being liked but as treatment moves from providing gratification to facing problems, being helped becomes as important as being liked. Adolescents are sensitive to emotional atmosphere and an adolescent will know if his counselor likes him without asking the question directly. A frequent meaning of the question is, "I am bad, how can anyone care about me?"

Anything that will arouse hope and expectation of gratification in the delinquent adolescent, even some forms of bribery, is valuable in the beginning of treatment. Such techniques may create therapeutic complications that will have to be worked out later, but this is less of a problem than refusal to return for treatment. Once the adolescent is engaged in a relationship, the counselor can then help foster genuine motivation for continuing.

In order to understand acting-out delinquent behavior it is necessary to go back to examine early aspects of ego growth. In the beginning months of life, in the early ego phase, the infant is geared toward one objective, direct gratification of impulse.

The nature of the gratifying object does not matter at first; the only significant point is that a gratifying object exists.

In normal development the infant begins to differentiate between and react to special persons. Controls are learned in relationship with, and in part through frustration by, important and significant individuals in the infant's life. Under certain traumatic developmental conditions which cause damage to the child's psyche, striving toward direct impulse gratification continues as the sole function of the ego without any controls imposed on this function. This can occur where there is excessive deprivation at an early age, or where there is excessive gratification of impulses without any concomitant development of the object relationships. If there is no parental interference with control of impulse the parents do not teach their children ways of dealing with their impulses. If he makes no demands or places no conditions in connection with gratification, the parent does not add an element of himself to the infant. The child has the constant fantasy of gratification but disregard for the parent as a person. Such a parent may be essentially cold or even cruel in his neglect of offering a personal relationship. The child settles for taking only, never giving, never being asked to give, never investing in another person. His gratifications come only through the use of people without personal involvement.

A child growing up under these circumstances is left without ways of managing his impulses. Because of hostility he will reject or rebel against the superego. The trauma causes rejection of the ego ideal of the family. This kind of traumatic developmental background produces delinquent acting-out impulse-ridden behavior. The impulse-ridden delinquent may respond to a re-educational process if treatment can be instituted early enough. He needs to be involved in a relationship which will be at first truly gratifying, and ultimately, educational, correcting the defects of his earlier development. The process is long and difficult.

There is another kind of development, nontraumatic, which

leads to delinquent impulse-ridden behavior. A child may become delinquent by growing up in a delinquent environment, by identification with delinquent parents and delinquent subcultural norms. His society imparts no control structure and his behavior is ego syntonic, that is totally acceptable to himself. The psychological and sociological problems involved are extremely difficult to handle in treatment. If it is possible to involve the individual in a satisfying relationship it may be possible to begin a long process of re-education to a different set of values.

But where the delinquency is characterologically deeply ingrained, with a superego which has developed in a delinquent style, the chances of success are not great. A counselor should however never assume too quickly that an adolescent is untreatable. Efforts must be made to engage the adolescent in a helping relationship that may be fruitful. If these efforts fail, however, it should be acknowledged that individual treatment is inadequate to bring about the desired changes for this kind of delinquent.

Adolescents whose acting-out behavior stems from participation in peer group activities may or may not require treatment. In some instances they may be normal adolescents only transiently engaged in antisocial acts with group sanction. Further investigation and study of the history will indicate whether the behavior is that of an ordinary adolescent or will reveal the diagnostic problems which underlie the acting out. The approach to the adolescent would then need to be based on the individual diagnostic findings.

Not uncommonly delinquent adolescents appear to be impulse-ridden when they actually are not. These adolescents may act as if they were without superegos. They quarrel with their parents and are difficult disciplinary problems at school. Sometimes they are irritable or brashly defiant. Even in treatment they may be insolent and unresponsive. Often the delinquent character formation is a defensive structure against a serious depression. It may be a depressive character disorder or a depressive psychosis.

It is difficult to determine in the beginning of treatment when direct gratification of impulse is being used defensively. The counselor whose bias prevents him from looking beyond the hostile symptomatic behavior will miss the underlying depression.

A detailed history is important and careful study of the information received from parents and others may give clues to the psychic conflicts. If the history reveals dependency deprivation, the ego can react to such deprivation by not taking on the values of the parents and their society. Or a child may have made desperate pleas for love and affection earlier in his life, tried excessive compliance to get approval, and when this failed, he may have developed a defensive cover with a delinquent pattern.

The counselor should be alert to the following symptoms and complaints, after medical examination has ruled out physical causes:

Overeating, loss of appetite or other dietary complaints;
Generalized feelings of illness, stomach or bowel disorder;
Apathy, irritability, or loss of zest and interest;
Sleep disturbances, such as insomnia or trouble falling asleep, disturbing dreams or waking too early, or fatigue during the day;
Insatiable longings for food, money, drugs, alcohol, gadgets, or sex. Such direct impulse gratification may also be a defense against the infantile impulses that realistically cannot be completely satisfied. The impulse is insatiable and the individual tries to get gratification from certain behavior such as gambling or stealing.

Sometimes these signs will have been ignored previously either because the adolescent does not like to admit his troubles or because the parents are not sympathetic or do not believe the distress is real. The delinquent behavior is so distressing in itself that it diverts attention from the adolescent's real underlying troubles. Its defensive purpose is to mask recognition of the inner difficulties from the adolescent himself. One delinquent boy who had been in treatment long enough to have established a good relationship with his counselor told him he smoked marijuana because "It helps to escape the hell inside me."

A delinquent who is actually defending against depression will also show the following evidence:

The impulses which are being acted on are not the most significant longings of the individual. For example, the adolescent may engage in meaningless destructive acts such as breaking windows or defacing walls.

In the past, the ego complied with an existing superego and did not always act on impulse. The history may indicate good behavior or compliance prior to the outbreak of the delinquent acts. Not infrequently parents will date the beginning of the delinquency at the start of high school which may often be equated with the onset of puberty.

The history may indicate an overly severe superego and a need for denial, rebellion or renunciation. Very severe moralistic or punitive parents often demand excessive compliance against which the adolescent may be rebelling.

Ego ideal considerations have only been put aside instead of being absent. An adolescent may say that he is not interested in school and sees no need for education. The adolescent however indicates that he is disturbed because he cannot study revealing that he does hold education as a value, but one with which he cannot at present comply.

The existence of an ongoing intrapsychic conflict of a neurotic nature. Usually this requires study for detection. For example, a boy with a severe castration anxiety may join a delinquent gang in order to overcome his fearfulness and prove to the world and to himself that he is strong and tough.

Since it is difficult at the outset to diagnose differentially between a corrupt or absent superego and a depression masked by delinquency, it is especially important to obtain a full history with special emphasis on ego and superego development. When a neurotic adolescent is seen shortly after an acting-out incident he may actually have a greater concern about his delinquent act than he displays in guilt or shame. A sensitive counselor who reacts to a feeling of the neurotic underlay may get a positive response when he expresses his interest sympathetically. Usually, however, the adolescent who is defending against depression will resist early attempts to uncover it, unlike the neurotic depressive who comes into treatment pleading for a close relationship.

But occasionally, surprisingly rapid breakthroughs occur when the counselor acts on his intuition of depressive underlay. A sixteen-year-old girl, referred for treatment because of promiscuous sexual acting out, blandly admitted the promiscuity but denied she had any problems. The only difficulty she felt lay in her parents' outmoded attitudes about sexual behavior. The counselor listened sympathetically and attentively, then cut through her defensive posture with a serious statement that her course of behavior inevitably indicated deep unhappiness. The girl's response was uncontrollable weeping.

It is therapeutically helpful to be optimistic about discovering a depression in approaching an acting-out delinquent. The treatment cannot lose and may gain by assuming that the delinquency is a cover for internal distress. An attitude of benign suspicion that the problem is depressive, combined with sympathy for the adolescent instead of condemnation for the delinquent act, serves to make the counselor more attentive to the subtle signs of the depression and orients him to a therapeutic rather than a punitive task.

The counselor relates to the unhappiness instead of to the

delinquency. He attempts to find the sources of the conflict and works toward getting the adolescent to recognize his own inner unhappiness. It then becomes possible to treat him as he would any troubled adolescent.

It may take many months for the adolescent to reach recognition of his conflicts and many more before he is ready to reveal them to the counselor, but without arriving at this point no real change can be accomplished. The treatment may have to be interrupted to wait until the adolescent is older and has suffered inwardly as well as in his environment before he is ready to accept help.

## THE OVER-COMPENSATED ADOLESCENT

A problem frequently seen is the adolescent boy who defends by overcompensation out of anxiety about heterosexuality, dependency or aggressive impulses. Boys who fear genuine competitive aggression may defend themselves against their fears by becoming overcompensated in areas where real aggression is not necessary. Overcompensated boys are often inhibited with girls and have castration anxiety. They may cover this inhibition by adopting a superficial exaggerated pseudo-masculine manner with girls.

Other desexualize their relationships, depreciate girls and affirm that they want nothing to do with them. They may immerse themselves in intellectual activities, important serious endeavors in contrast to what they term the frivolity of boy-girl relationships.

Out of anxiety over aggressiveness some overcompensated boys are counterphobic and may engage in aggressive acts even though they are fearful. This maneuver is probably healthier than retreat but the helping task is still to deal with the basic issues of the underlying anxieties.

Many types of dynamics can create overcompensation. Because of the wide range which can result in similar defensive outcomes, the counselor must understand why the defenses have become necessary to the individual and how a particular anxiety or piece of behavior has evolved.

A boy may have conflict because his father was the affectionate tender parent in his family. At first this closeness to the father is acceptable but it makes the need for a loving father especially significant. Later, as the child grows and his psychic life becomes elaborated, his feelings of love involve his genitalia so that memories of physical intimacy with the father acquire a sexual connotation. But the child may also learn that such feelings for father are "bad" or "not nice" and the feelings then become unacceptable and are repressed. The feelings are labeled weak or feminine. For overcompensated boys life has exaggerated this issue. They grow up believing that they must be tough or strong and they find it especially difficult to discover in themselves soft warm affectionate feelings for another male either in the present, in the treatment relationship, or earlier in their lives.

Some boys overcompensate to defend against identification with their mothers. A boy will identify with his father if the father loved his son even though the father, from any objective point of view, does not have the desirable qualifications that make him a good source of identification. On the other hand, a child who received no love from his father may turn to the more loving, more adequate mother as a source of identification. He may not necessarily identify with the mother's femininity, but only with those qualities within her that he admires, such as her strength.

Nevertheless, there is a general tendency to confuse the sexual with the nonsexual and the boy may have anxiety about being feminine because of his strong identification with his mother. Whether the boy has actually taken on a feminine character, or only has anxiety that he may have, he may be impelled to overcompensate in order to make himself feel more adequate.

An added problem may arise if school achievement is identified with femininity. Often in less educated subcultures, school achievement is considered a female characteristic. Even more generally, school represents a female activity, extending perhaps from the fact that female teachers predominate in the lower grades. American history and folklore traditionally label education and refinement effete; the heroes are strong and tough, too busy with action for book learning.

In a family where the mother depreciates the father, the mother can convey to her son that a real man would not be like the father. If the father is nonintellectual, the mother may prize educational achievement in her son. The boy can come to feel that the mother's affection is given on the basis of this school achievement, and such a boy may take on an exaggerated overcompensated interest in intellectual activities.

Often the fathers of overcompensated boys are depreciated and weak, with the mother the stronger parent. The mother makes it clear she values highly masculine strengths in her son. In order to gain and hold his mother's love the boy feels he must try to be unlike his father, even though he may have identified with his father. He resolves his conflict by ridiculing his father which is also a projection of the same weakness in himself. Since male figures are objects of ridicule to this boy, he will also need to depreciate his male counselor.

When overcompensated adolescent boys move into a meaningful relationship with a male counselor (and male counselors are almost essential for them) they often associate the warm relationship with femininity and the dependency on a male with homosexuality. They feel emasculated and need to rebuild the overcompensatory defenses. For these boys, liking the counselor and revealing their inadequacies to him create feelings of weakness and reactivate dependency wishes against which they defend. How serious a problem this may be in treatment is an individual matter determined by how much conflict exists around the dependency. With each situation special factors in the individual history account for the struggle.

The overcompensated boy will experience negative affects of shame because he feels like a girl when he feels close to his counselor. In treatment, theoretically, the first step should be to overcome the negative affect, but in practice it is often intertwined with the exploration of why the boy came to feel so inadequate. Exploration in itself helps overcome the negative. When the counselor says, "Let's find out how this came about," the neutral nonanxious manner is reassuring and the task of exploration becomes less threatening. Many adolescents need an explicit kind of reassurance about negative affects before they can proceed. The treatment cannot lose by reassurance. "This is not an uncommon feeling." "Lots of boys feel this way."

The issues of dependency are more easily handled therapeutically if they are first brought up by the adolescent. The technique again is to reassure through common-sense interpretation about the meanings of relationships and the need for closeness as part of ordinary human feeling.

Since at the outset of treatment many overcompensated adolescents deny they have any difficulties the first step is to get the adolescent to accept that his behavior is exaggerated. The therapeutic purpose is to relieve the anxiety and the basic conflicts, not merely to change the overcompensated behavior. The counselor will need to gain understanding of the special developmental issues out of which the overcompensatory defenses arose.

Once the adolescent is solidly engaged in treatment he may himself raise the issues against which he had at first defended himself. When he is able to admit some of his own concerns the counselor helps him to elaborate and to explore his feelings. Usually special anxieties will be uncovered about dependence, aggression, or sexuality. As a further step the counselor directs attention to what brought about such feelings and their defenses. For example, after a boy has admitted that he is indeed afraid of authority the counselor can tell him that the fear is what makes it necessary for him to act destructively or rebelliously and can add that the behavior does not really solve the problem. In this way the original defensiveness gradually becomes unnecessary.

Treatment moves when the adolescent brings up and elaborates the inadequacies which cause him to be anxious and afraid. At that point he has given up the defensive façade and treatment can advance to the real issue of help with the feelings.

The ultimate step in treatment is correction of the conflict that created the particular anxiety. The therapeutic goal is reached at the point when the defense no longer causes trouble in the life of the adolescent and when the remaining conflicts are not too great for him to tolerate. If conflicts have decreased and the adolescent can live in relative comfort with modified defenses, the treatment goals will have been accomplished even if the adolescent continues to operate in a somewhat overcompensated manner.

A counselor may decide not to touch on some forms of overcompensation; if the defense does not cause difficulty in the environment and if the adolescent is not greatly concerned about his overcompensated behavior, the treatment may ignore this defense. Generally, it is the adolescent himself who determines the focus of treatment. For example, an adolescent may be studying very hard as an expression of overcompensation but help is not indicated if the adolescent himself is not disturbed about what he is doing. An inhibited boy studying very hard and doing well in school might be afraid of girls, but specific attempts to change the overcompensation would not be appropriate if he was not yet ready to be involved with girls and was not troubled by this lack in his life.

Ordinarily adolescents are not brought into treatment because they study too hard yet such behavior may be a defensive overcompensation against feelings of inferiority or even worthlessness. But when an adolescent comes because of another difficulty the counselor may observe that overcompensation exists and consider its dynamics in relation to the rest of the personality. The counselor however will be cautious in undoing this defensive overcompensation with the adolescent for fear of arousing depression or too much anxiety. A patient counselor, working cautiously, will help modify the overcompensation without directly approaching the overcompensatory defenses themselves.

## DEALING WITH HOMOSEXUAL FEELINGS

Among the most difficult concerns adolescents have to deal with are homosexual feelings and the anxieties about these feelings. Although few adolescents are overtly homosexual, there are many who engage in some homosexual play as an outcome of the developmental experimental process. Even those who do not actually take part in any overt homosexual activity feel anxious about their heterosexuality. Homosexual feelings and concerns about them are almost universal in adolescence. These feelings are often aroused by the close relationship to the counselor. The counselor needs the utmost sensitivity, dexterity of technique and skill in timing to be able to help the young adolescent handle anxiety about homosexual feelings.

Adolescent boys are extremely distressed when they believe they may be homosexual. Interestingly enough, they do not have the same anxiety about certain homosexual activities, such as playing with or comparing each others' genitals, or even engaging in fellatio if they find a cooperative partner. These activities may be considered by the peer group actually as a display of proof of masculinity.

When adolescent boys have had experiences of homosexual activities which they see as masculine, they are able to discuss the activities with the counselor. But they have great difficulty talking if they fear they have homosexual feelings. Older adolescents often come into treatment because of anxiety about homosexual feelings. But high school adolescents will usually deny or repress such feelings; they may experience some sexual feelings about their counselor but express them mainly in terms of dependency or receptive needs. To be in treatment is to want something from the counselor. Most adolescent boys shy away from bringing any of these feelings into the open especially if they have sexual connotation.

Girls are much less concerned than boys about closeness to others of the same sex. It is culturally accepted for girls to hug or kiss each other. They do not consider the physical intimacies which they enjoy in pajama parties or dancing with each other as sexual. Girls talk freely about love and loving. They accept these feelings as natural and they do not have the same fears and anxieties about them as do boys who equate them with weakness. But adolescent girls are still frightened by any implications of homosexuality in these feelings.

The counselor should be careful about the use of the term homosexual, usually interpreted as sexual perversion. Adolescents, and even adults, have often been frightened away from treatment by a comment which indicates a homosexual problem.

Homolibidinal is a more accurate word for the feelings adolescents develop for their counselor. Homolibidinal feelings may be expressed in sexual terms as homosexual fantasy, or as neutralized fondness for a person of the same sex. Some aspects of these feelings merely represent a need for affection from a person of the same sex.

Most adolescents are so frightened of these feelings that they are only brought up in relation to another person, displaced from the counselor, if they are discussed at all. Reassuring comments about the universality of these feelings can be made when the counselor picks up the anxiety even if the adolescent does not directly discuss it. The adolescent can be told that what he is really saying is that a certain person is important to him and that what he feels is affection even though he feels it as if it were sexual. This kind of comment is both reassuring and clinically accurate. It is particularly important and useful with adolescents who have any paranoid tendencies since they become extremely distressed by the idea of homosexuality.

The counselor bypasses the more narrow sexual components in the feelings of the adolescent for another person of the same sex by emphasizing the universal need for love and affection. He clarifies the adolescent's misconceptions about sexual identity and the confusions that lead him to feel certain activities or feelings or behavior belong exclusively to one sex or are homosexual. This kind of reassurance does not abolish fantasies about homosexuality but the counselor's understanding acceptance of the real meaning of the feelings will help lessen the anxiety.

There are adolescents with homosexual problems and these must be dealt with in terms of the specific dynamics involved. These adolescents, after some initial anxieties about self-revelation, may discuss their homosexual tendencies or even overt homosexuality. Because the personality is not yet solidly fixed in adolescence, it is extremely important for the counselor to attempt to help the adolescent alter these forces within his character which have led him to a homosexual resolution. Not every adolescent who has experienced overt homosexual activity develops into an adult homosexual. When the usual helping attempts fail to alter the homosexual tendency and there is evidence that the adolescent character structure is settling into homosexuality, more intensive treatment or perhaps psychoanalysis is indicated.

### AFFECT PROBLEMS

The feeling life of the adolescent is intense. During the adolescent years the affects are probably more easily aroused, more labile and more poignant than at any other period in life. Adolescence is the age of acute suffering and ecstatic happiness, of vivid sensitivity to pain and to beauty, the age of the dire tragedy and the grand passion.

Affect is a highly complex psychic process. Developmentally, sensations and feelings, which are body phenomena, precede the complicated psychic experience termed affect. A hungry infant cries; he experiences vascular and motor reactions of hunger and the sensations of crying. Then his mother appears to soothe and feed him. The child undergoes a definite sequence: hunger, crying, cuddling, feeding. These all occur around an object, the mother, and begin to establish an affect state in connection with the need for the mother. A child learns to recognize the gestalt of impulse, body sensation and object; this interrelated complex is affect. After the development of language, the child gives verbal labels to many affects. Rage, love and fear are the basic affects and exist primitively. Shame, pride, annoyance, distaste and many others are modifications of the early primitive affects. By the time of adolescence an individual has acquired an extensive repertoire of affective experience.

Defenses against affect arise from the ego's need to manage impulse. The type of affect may indicate the basic impulse involved. The affect of desire may indicate the sexual impulse; rage, the impulse to destroy. Most affects, however, are the final result of a more complex psychodynamic flow within the individual. The affect of guilt, for example, is the outcome of the ego's turning the impulse of hostility onto itself and the internalized anticipation of punishment by the parents. It may include various sensations, gnawing in the upper abdomen, feelings of being heavy-laden, or wanting to inflict self-punishment such as kicking one's self or pulling one's hair.

Love, too, is not a simple experience of a single impulse. It is composed of positive anticipation of many kinds of gratification, pregenital and genital, modified by what the individual ego needs from people in his life.

Most affect states, therefore, are not simple expressions of the original impulse but are complex modifications and redirections. Affects are among the most important inner experiences in life. Much effort in treatment is directed toward getting people to re-experience affects. It is accordingly important to recognize when defenses against affect exist. The need to defend against affect depends on whether the experience of the affect is acceptable or unacceptable to the individual. A person can also displace his affect or produce another kind of affect instead of the original, such as bursts of laughter instead of crying. These represent modifications of the pure defense against affect. Affects may themselves be used as defense. One affect may be a defense against another, as for instance, irritation as a defense against a show of affection.

### Blocking of Affect

A common defense against affect is blocking, not feeling an affect which should exist.

Affect is the *conscious experience* which most closely relates to original impulse. The conscious experience of rage is related to the impulse, at the deepest level, of wanting to destroy the offending person. This impulse asks for discharge into action in which the object of the rage is to be destroyed. The idea accompanying this experience may be to strike out at the offender. The action taken will depend on many factors, on the reality circumstances, and on how the ego controls or permits discharge. But the affect of anger indicates that the impulse exists, and is as close as people get to experiencing the impulse itself. Therefore, blocking the affect is an attempt to block the impulse. Some people have been taught that feelings of anger are unacceptable so that the motivation for blocking the anger may be the affect itself; the anger, not merely the original impulse, is unacceptable.

When affect is blocked, the conscious experience is that the affect does not exist. An incident which should result in rage arouses no conscious feeling. But unconsciously the affect continues to exist because it is derived from the impulse.

Adolescents may block affects because the intensity is so great and often so unacceptable that the feelings cause acute shame or embarrassment. Frequently what seems like nonchalance, brazenness, or callousness in an adolescent is the outcome of blocking unacceptable affects.

## Mood Alterations

Quick changes of affect are frequently seen in adolescents. The alteration of mood occurs because the adolescent ego cannot tolerate a particular feeling and swings to an opposite for defensive purposes.

Extreme unpredictable swings of affect indicate excessive reactivity. Adolescents whose personality structures are infantile and labile and whose egos are insufficiently controlling of their behavior are those most likely to show extreme swings of affect. The ego cannot stop the affect changes, and it is not precisely known what deficit in the ego permits the swings to take place. In the most extreme forms, affect swings are present in manic-depressive psychoses.

Mood swings, a milder manifestation, occur in healthier adolescents. More ego control is involved in the change of mood than in affect swings.

A high school girl may become very angry with her mother who refuses permission to date on a school night. The girl shows her anger by shouting and breaks a dish in rushing off from the dinner table. Her mother is understanding about the anger and tries to soothe her. The girl then becomes quiet and depressed. Later in the evening she dances in an exaggerated way to her records and giggles inappropriately at anything that is said to her. The sequence in this series of occurrences is as follows: the hostility to her mother is so great that it is necessary to defend against it by turning the hostility inward; guilt and depression result. Because guilt is an unpleasant affect to sustain, the girl then defends herself against this feeling and her affect swings to the opposite direction, to hypomania as defense against the guilt. None of this is a conscious process; the hostility is denied.

The hostility to the object (the mother) and to her edicts are also denied. What may develop is indifference, nonchalance or playfulness, the attitude that nothing serious or dangerous or worth being discouraged about has happened. Instead the adolescent may become exuberant or even euphoric.

The affect swings of adults and adolescents have little fundamental dynamic difference. Adults are likely to be more profoundly depressed in a depressed phase than adolescents who are more hopeful even when they are depressed. There is cultural acceptance of moodiness in adolescents so that alternating affects and shifting moods are not regarded as being as unusual for them as for adults. Adolescents tend to feel that depression is a disturbed state more readily than adults do. While parents and others expect to see changeable behavior in an adolescent, with variations from sadness and discouragement to excitability and enthusiasm, the persistence of either a depressed or a euphoric state usually causes concern.

Depression is more serious for an adult than for an adolescent for the following reasons: (1) even when depressed, the adolescent retains more involvement; (2) in depression the adolescent feels less hopeless; (3) the adolescent is generally more labile, his depression lifts more quickly and he has the capacity for more rapid mood changes; (4) even in depression adolescents are more physically active than adults; they have more energy available. Superficially, it appears that a depression may be set off in an adolescent by less significant precipitating factors than for adults. An adolescent may become depressed over disappointing grades, or a trivial argument with people important in his life. But, from the viewpoint of the adolescent these are as important as the death of a loved one or a business failure which may precipitate depression in an adult.

The adolescent may show more dramatic reaction in a depression than an adult who is often able to tolerate depression for a long period of time without actually showing it. Even during the depression not all of the hostility is internalized in adolescents. Some anger is directed against external objects.

Adolescent girls are more inclined to become passive and languid during depression than boys. The basic psychodynamic cause for depression has to do with the early relationship with the mother. Since girls are deeply involved with and identified with their mothers, they have a somewhat greater struggle in depressions than do boys. However, even lethargic depressed adolescent girls show more physical activity than depressed women.

Mood swings and depression are serious symptoms. The conflicts are profound and have their origin in a very early phase of life. Treatment techniques are based on the recognition that unconsciously the adolescent is trying to re-establish his early infantile dependent relationship which may include destructive incorporation fantasies.

The depressed adolescent unconsciously expects to incorporate the counselor. The adolescent's fantasy of incorporation equates with destruction; the counselor can use a variety of techniques to prove that in reality the counselor is not destroyed but remains available for the adolescent in spite of such fantasies.

The adolescent with an affect disorder wants the counselor to gratify his infantile wishes and needs almost infantile closeness. The counselor permits the immediacy of the relationship to provide closeness in an acceptable way. The counselor therefore should be relaxed about engaging in professionally appropriate physical contact. By shaking hands, or placing a hand on the adolescent's shoulder in greeting or farewell the close emotional relationship is symbolically established. It is appropriate and may be helpful for the counselor to offer candy, cookies or soft drinks. By his manner the counselor conveys that the relationship with the adolescent is a predictable and constant one, assuring the adolescent that he will not lose the counselor no matter what his hostile fantasies. He also attempts to indicate that destruction does not result from the adolescent's hostile feelings. Through his dependability the counselor proves to the adolescent that incorporation of the maternal figure does not destroy the mother.

## SUICIDE

Suicide is an extreme expression of introversion of hostility in depression. If the superego is very punitive, and if the hostile impulses are strong, the ego may feel that the pressures to commit suicide are too great to resist.

Almost all adolescents think about suicide at times and may talk about it, but usually suicide is attempted only by seriously depressed adolescents. Their great hope, and the push of life force, act as deterrents except in severe pathology. Adolescent psychotics may commit suicide out of bizarre interpretations of reality. Any threat of suicide however should be taken seriously by an adolescent's family and counselor.

Because of the resurgence of impulse, the adolescent is geared toward action, has less potential for delay or control of action than an adult, even though the adolescent may not be as seriously depressed clinically as an adult who delays self-destructive action. Just as seemingly trivial occurrences, poor grades, slight rejection by friends, minor family quarrels may precipitate adolescent depressions, suicides too, may be triggered by what appears insignificant to an adult. It is for this reason that the counselor must be concerned about the suicidal potential of any depressed adolescent.

Adolescent suicides sometimes occur as the result of dramatic hysterical gestures, intended to affect the environment rather than to destroy the self by death. They may be accidental in the sense that the adolescent did not intend to carry the suicide gesture to its ultimate conclusion.

## INHIBITION

Inhibition is a defense against the discharge of an impulse; the impulse is not acted upon but is held back, usually as an outcome of repression. Impulses always tend toward discharge in motor activities, muscular or glandular; they also find discharge in fantasy and in dreams. The ego can unconsciously inhibit bodily or muscular functioning so that there is not the same degree of discharge of impulse in affect or motor activity. Also, the ego may unconsciously inhibit fantasy life in a similar way. Finally, inhibition can be more generalized so as to be characterological.

The intensification of impulses during adolescence, and the strength of sexual urges prompt the use of inhibition in those adolescents with strong superegos. But the inhibition of the adolescent is usually inconsistent. At times an adolescent may find himself unable to approach a member of the opposite sex even to exchange ordinary greetings. Yet at other times the adolescent will experience a shocking breakthrough of feeling and action which fills him with shame and guilt. The suddenness and crudeness with which this happens is an indication of the fluctuating controls of impulse. The adolescent ego experiences pressure to fulfill the longings of the intense urges.

In some adolescents inhibitions pervade the behavior and there can be no breakthrough. In those instances, the extent of the shyness and social awkwardness is a measure of the intensity of inhibition.

An inhibition which keeps an adolescent from getting into trouble, from being too destructive or hypersexual, may serve him well during early adolescence. In general, because of cultural dictates and biological considerations, counselors have less question about helping adolescent boys overcome sexual inhibitions than girls.

### Characterological Inhibition

Inhibitions can pervade the total character so that an adolescent is meek, passive and unassertive in many different situations. An inhibited adolescent whose character formation mainly arises out of the oedepal phase of development will have a great deal of energy and libido. The action may be inhibited but there may be considerable fantasy life and a great discharge of energy in ideation but not in action. Usually inhibited adolescents find other ways to express affect. They may engage in a rich fantasy life with minimal action, like Walter Mitty in the Thurber story. Or an adolescent so characterologically inhibited that he cannot interact personally with others may put his energies into his school work or into some creative or artistic field.

The characterologically inhibited adolescent may at first resemble an individual with an inadequate ego, with little available energy; but the extent of the fantasy life, or of the enthusiasm in any area, differentiates the inhibited from the inadequate. An adolescent may be sufficiently inhibited to give the surface appearance of a schizoid character. But there are important differences. The inhibited adolescent, in contrast to the schizoid, sees the world accurately. Also there are sufficient indications in the inhibited character that affect is present and appropriate; the affect *almost* expresses itself although it never manages to do so freely.

A counselor will feel the strange quality in a schizoid, the inappropriateness, the distortion of the response instead of the restrained response of the inhibited adolescent. The differences become more apparent as treatment continues. The schizoid adolescent creates an atmosphere of distance and strangeness; the inhibited does not. He invokes empathy in the counselor instead of the predominant sense of alienation felt in the presence of the schizoid.

In treatment, the characterological inhibition will undergo some loosening and some breakthrough of energy will take place, either in action or in fantasy. Treatment deals with the defenses to free the impulses so that they may then be handled in more effective and less neurotic ways. On the other hand, the treatment of an adolescent with an inadequate ego is essentially supportive and educative with no attempts to uncover or undo the defensive structure necessary for the maintenance of stability. It is because of the gerat difference in treatment techniques that it is essential to formulate diagnostic differentials between the inhibited and the adolescent with an inadequate ego.

## PASSIVITY

Passivity is one of the most common defenses in adolescence and it is also one of the most difficult to deal with. There are two kinds of passive defenses, aggressive and non-aggressive. Both are active processes of adaptation even though the external manifestations are passive.

The defense of passivity arises from anxieties having to do with aggression and action. The conflict centers about the fact that the child feels that to be aggressively active is dangerous. The danger may lie in fear of the activity itself or fear of punishment as a consequence of the activity. Sometimes activity is equated with competition and destructiveness. Therefore the child fears competition and retreats into passivity.

However, this adaptation may also be an attempt to fulfill the infantile wish for complete gratification without active participation which arises from infancy when the ego had minimal participation and the mother provided for all needs, or from a fantasy of complete gratification such as the satiated sleep of an infant. Although even the ego of the sleeping infant engages in some activity, maintaining body posture or dreaming, voluntary efforts are minimal and the fantasy touches on the attempt to reinstate the possibility of fulfillment without voluntary ego action.

The non-aggressive passive adolescent does not directly cause trouble because he does not involve himself in any activity. He *does* very little. In treatment he will not talk freely to his counselor, will not ask questions, and will have little to say about his problems. In school, he does not participate in the classroom, is not interested in school work, may not complete assignments, takes no part in extra-curricular activities. At home the adolescent sits around doing nothing, has to be reminded to carry out routine chores, and may even need to be called to the table for meals.

The aggressive type of passive adolescent manifestly is much like the nonaggressive passive adolescent but the different quality of the passivity can be sensed. Instead of a lack of enthusiasm and spontaneity, there is purposeful and energetic stubbornness. The non-aggressive passive adolescent who does not do his homework seems to have no interest in doing the assignment, but the aggressive type shows covert defiance in *positively* not doing the work. In contrast to the general lack of interest in the non-aggressive adolescent, the passive-aggressive adolescent may be interested in many things. He will not read his textbooks but may read other books. He will not do his math problems but may do complicated figuring in relation to baseball statistics. The passive-aggressive adolescent may be active outside of class and have fun with his peers. This type of passivity may show itself only in certain areas.

A difficult therapeutic problem exists with adolescents who use the defense of aggressive passivity. The ego uses this defense almost voluntarily in a stubborn, defiant hostile manner; the ego is *active* in maintaining passivity. The dynamics involve recognition, in some ways close to consciousness, that other people, usually the parents, expect and value activity. Since the adolescent recognizes this, his purpose is to frustrate the parent, to be hostile, vengeful and retaliatory.

Aggressive passivity originates in strong ego capacities partly related to early experiences of biting and the awareness that the muscles of the jaw are powerful but chiefly to early anal activities. The ego discovers early that these are activities which the parents cannot control since the resistance can be expressed with musculature inaccessible to the parents.

Inhibited adolescents often seem passive but they tend to want to carry on activity. The ego effort of wishing to do something and the restraint that makes them unable to act are strong enough to be sensed. For example, an inhibited girl, sitting on the sidelines at a party, will want to participate and her anxiety about being unable to do so is communicated to a sensitive observer. A non-aggressive passive girl will merely sit, waiting for whatever might happen, without observable anxiety.

The quality of passivity is different in adolescents than in adults. The passively defiant adolescent manifests the defense more openly. An adult who does nothing has to rationalize his passivity and is disturbed about it. It is not consciously ego-syntonic as it may be with the adolescent. The reason for this difference stems from life experience. The world requires activity and adults learn that passivity involves serious consequences, such as losing employment. The adolescent does not yet appreciate the consequences of his behavior and tends to remain passive with impunity and a "so what?" attitude.

Also, the reality of life circumstances allows an adolescent to postpone the need to do anything about his passivity. Even some older adolescents give in to this mode of behavior, though reality may become harsh, as when parents decide they will not provide support any longer. Such adolescents may try a drifter's life, working minimally at unskilled jobs. But for high school adolescents reality is not so pressing since their parents carry the responsibility for their maintenance.

Some adolescents, together with the passivity, have a corruptive, manipulative ability; they can get teachers to pass them by seductive manipulations, although they have not done the work. Many manipulative adolescents who seem to get by with doing nothing are actually deeply angry. They feel they have received nothing from their parents and are getting revenge for their basic deprivation. In some instances, there may be depression underlying this attitude. Their only expectation from relationships is to be given to materially; they give to others only as a bribe. Universally, relationships develop out of the experience of having been given to, and people all through life equate the giving and receiving of gifts with love. But passive adolescents who manipulate have despaired of receiving love and can value only what they can manage to get materially and concretely from others.

Treatment of passive adolescents begins with the establishment of a dependent relationship. They must be fed, literally and symbolically (actually and emotionally) for a long time in the hope that this feeding will ultimately create the same dependent feelings for the counselor that an infant feels for the mother on whom he depends for food.

These adolescents must be met on whatever basis they can accept, particularly in the beginning phase of treatment. Giving to them is an important aspect of treatment. The treatment aims to arrive at the point where the adolescent wants to be liked by his counselor. From that point, perhaps, the adolescent may begin to do better in school or elsewhere on the basis of gaining approval.

The treatment course is long and arduous but it is this early phase of treatment with the passive adolescent that is most crucial.

# 9

# Termination of Treatment

AT THE OUTSET of treatment goals are formulated based on the individual needs and capacity of the particular adolescent. Ideally counselor and adolescent agree, in a therapeutic alliance, on the focus of treatment and the eventual aims. During the course of treatment various factors may indicate changes either in the major focus or in the extent to which it is possible to achieve the goals. The goals must be realistically set; treatment cannot promise resolution of all conflict.

Under the most fortunate circumstances, termination takes place when the problems for which the adolescent came into treatment have been resolved. But human personality is complex and therapeutic techniques for altering personality are limited. The counselor needs to determine how much change or how much alleviation can realistically be expected and when this point has been reached.

In a physical illness the patient is discharged when the complaint has been alleviated. Treatment of personality disorders encompasses more than relief of complaints; it also aims at the resolution of inner conflict and changes in modes of behavior. Symptoms in personality disorder are not easily relieved. They persist because they are the superficial, outer manifestations of inner volcanic processes. As long as these processes continue inside, the symptoms persist. Many times although the symptom

160

is the conscious reason for seeking treatment there may be a greater variety of malfunctioning and psychic distress than is evident in the original complaint.

Relief of complaints alone is not an adequate goal because the symptoms may return upon termination of treatment. But the counselor may in some instances consider termination when symptoms have been moderated because this may be all that can be accomplished. In other cases there may be modification of the personality although specific symptoms may persist. The improvement in personality may be sufficient reason for the counselor to consider termination but the adolescent may protest. He may want alleviation of the original complaint, and while this is valid, treatment cannot always fulfill this wish.

A defense is not necessarily given up because a person knows what his defense is, is conscious of it, or even understands its motivation or the dynamics behind it. There may be resistance to change; basically the term resistance means that a certain defense continues. There are many reasons why defenses continue and habituation is one. For example, an adolescent may continue to suffer acute stage fright even after he knows that it arose originally beause of fear of parental disapproval of exhibitionism. People continue to fear their impulses and the consequences they feel may follow, even when they have gained understanding of the dynamics of the defense. Hopefully, treatment will dilute the anxieties so that they may be better tolerated.

The counselor must determine how much treatment can achieve and what further modifications or allevations can realistically be expected if it continues.

If the adolescent has accepted the degree of relief he has achieved and the counselor believes that some alteration has been accomplished, both adolescent and counselor can be in agreement that sufficient changes have occurred for treatment to terminate.

When agreement is reached a definite time for termination is set with the adolescent. It is helpful if this time can coincide with some realistic event, such as the end of the school year or term, a vacation period, for either the adolescent or the counselor, or a specific holiday which makes a natural break in the continuity of appointments.

The remainder of the treatment then, is concerned with separation anxieties, the issues of dependence, functioning independently and giving up dependent gratifications, real and fantasied. The universal reluctance to give up gratification tends to make for a recurrence of difficulties during the terminal period. The regressions are an expression of the unwillingness to give up the counselor. To an adolescent, separating from the relationship means growing up, losing gratifying childhood fantasies. His anxieties around the questions whether he can become an adult and can manage as adults do, cause regression and recurrence of symptoms. The counselor must be aware of this, must understand why symptoms recur, but his concern during the terminal phase will not be with the symptoms precipitated by the prospect of ending, but with the fears about leaving.

When a reasonably secure decision has been reached about the accomplishment of the original goals, the final phase of treatment is devoted to the meaning of termination. It is important that the counselor not get lost in the details of the problems the adolescent will bring at this time. Instead the adolescent should be directed to his feelings about the impending separation.

Relevant issues of dependence and independence will already have been handled in treatment; in the termination phase the counselor corrects the adolescent's misconceptions in his fantasies about the meaning of giving up childhood and becoming an adult. He will bolster the adolescent's independence, will emphasize the fact that he has already been functioning on his own, not only relying on the counselor's help.

Termination means separation and separation is usually accompanied by ambivalent feelings. When termination of treatment is suggested, the growth implied, the achievement attained and the hopes for the future are all on the positive side of the ambivalent balance. But the negative side includes the pain of separation and all of the defensive reactions to avoid that pain. The termination phase provides a time for working through some of these problems. Specific memories about separation experiences may be reawakened, deaths, separations from loved ones, or loss of parents. Much of this may be seen in transference to the counselor and can be interpreted on this basis.

In the terminating phase also, new material frequently comes to light. The counselor must remember that the stimulus for the new material is the impending termination. But this gives an opportunity to work out issues not previously introduced. If anxiety does not lessen, the final termination date may be extended, with clear understanding that the remainder of the treatment is directed toward ending. If the anxiety is not great, even though the adolescent still desires to cling, the original termination date is adhered to. The adolescent is told that he can come back at a later time if he desires. He can also be told that his anxiety will diminish as he gives himself a chance to function on his own. Unconsciously, all separations are seen as final but realistically there is nothing irreversible about termination of treatment. The adolescent can always return if further help is needed.

The problems of termination are increased when the adolescent does not agree to termination. The counselor may know that he is functioning better, but the adolescent claims that he does not feel better. The problem then is to make the adolescent aware of the areas of improvement and to try to work out why he insists that he has not improved. This leads into specific issues. Often there is reluctance to give up the dependent relationship. The adolescent will maintain symptoms in order to hold onto the counselor. The problems may be serious ones which the adolescent indicates he still wants to work out. The counselor must make the decision as to whether anything further can be accomplished with these problems. The adolescent can be asked how much time he feels he needs and some definite further period of time can be allotted for the problem solving.

When the counselor has decided little more can be accomplished, some reconciliation must be made with a dissatisfied or reluctant adolescent. Acceptance of limitation and continued endurance of pain or discomfort is hard for anyone. It is especially hard for an adolescent to reconcile himself to the fact that some of his problems may continue. The counselor can realistically give him hope that there will be further changes as life goes on. There is abatement of issues in adulthood which were troublesome in adolescence. There is less libidinal push in adults; the defenses which were in flux in adolescence tend to settle and conflicts are resolved. An adult may have regrets about his limitations but he does not suffer over them with the agony of the adolescent. The process of acceptance may be an adaptation, a defensive resolution, but the adult can function more smoothly as a result of it. In termination the counselor attempts to get the adolescent to achieve a partial adult acceptance.

The adolescent who does not wish to terminate will deny that there have been changes or improvements. Real personality change takes time; alterations are not always immediately visible. When some worth-while goals have been achieved, the adolescent should be urged to try to function on his own. Self-sufficiency leads to integration of personality. Prolonged reliance upon the counselor may interfere with spontaneous personality changes in adolescence.

When the adolescent's disagreement with the suggestion of termination has been overcome, then the problems of separation anxiety, fear of adulthood, reluctance to give up gratifying dependency, and so forth, must be dealt with, just as in those instances where termination has been mutually agreed on. And again, the door is left open for return to treatment.

More often, however, adolescents tend to want to give up treatment and try to be on their own. This is especially true of the healthier personalities. The life of the adolescent is still future-oriented. It encompasses stages in growth, steps in the business of living, such as graduation, beginning employment or college. Adolescents keep looking forward toward a future in which there will be gratification and any progressive steps toward achievement tend to make them wish to give up treatment. The termination of treatment, too, may be seen as one of these end points or new beginnings.

In most cases the counselor will support the positives involved in termination. The counselor will consider the reality factors and the emotional state of the adolescent to determine if the reasons are a flight from treatment. A decision to go away to school may be flight but it is usually not wise to interfere unless the adolescent is seriously disturbed. Otherwise he should be encouraged to try living away from home and from treatment.

When an adolescent wishes to terminate although the counselor does not believe he is ready, the counselor should think through what has already been resolved and what remains to be worked out, what the current circumstances are and how much more can realistically be accomplished. Searching inquiry on the part of the counselor is called for into his own personal gratifications in the relationship. He must think through the countertransference issues to determine why it has not occurred to him that the adolescent is ready to terminate.

When transfer to another counselor is being considered, either because the counselor or adolescent will be in another city, there should first be careful thinking through of what has already been accomplished and how much further alleviation can be hoped for.

When termination is forced because parents wish to withdraw the adolescent, little can be hoped for in reversing the decision. The counselor can try to convince the parents that the adolescent should be permitted to remain in treatment. But even if this brings reluctant permission for continuance there is always the danger that the parents will sabotage treatment, either consciously or unconsciously. When termination does take place under these circumstances it deals with the same issues as endings under more favorable conditions, separation anxiety, dependency issues.

The passage of time is a factor in termination of treatment for adolescents. An adolescent may need more life experience before continued treatment can produce further changes. He may need added years in order to see that it is his own personality which operates to cause difficulties, not his father or his mother or others. Time may show him that his opposition to the adult world may be a process of fighting windmills of his own creation.

During adolescence the personality tends toward synthesis, the settling of unconscious psychodynamic issues. Treatment is directed toward undoing poor syntheses and creating better ones. With or without treatment the process of settling goes on in adolescence, internally and externally. It occurs when certain conflictual issues find their resolution within the total personality. The growth push from early to late adolescence aids the process. Synthesis is promoted by external factors, sometimes with dramatic suddenness. For example, an adolescent boy may decide he no longer needs treatment because he has acquired a girl friend. The pleasurable relationship with the girl has resolved some issues for him and his personality synthesis has taken a definite direction toward its adult form. The same leap forward occurs with a change of school, a firm decision about vocational goals, or any of a number of outside reality factors. The adolescent has come upon a solution and he may then feel ready to terminate treatment.

The counselor should be alert to indications that an adolescent is ready to try functioning independently and should not foster prolonged clinging. Handled skillfully, the process of termination is in itself therapeutic, offering opportunity for further resolution of the universal anxieties about separation and the conflicts about dependence.

# 10

## Transference and Countertransference

THE PRINCIPLE of transference is repetition in the present of feelings, attitudes and behavior carried over from the reactions to parents or parent surrogates in the past.

An adult who enters treatment ordinarily has repressed episodes from the past and in the present usually is dealing with his parents as one adult deals with another. In treatment, the old traumas may be revived and the adult may then transfer to his counselor feelings which belong to the earlier relationship with his parents.

In contrast, adolescents who are in treatment usually are living with their parents; current interactions are taking place between them, and the adolescent realistically remains in the role of a child in his family. The adolescent has had traumas in the past which have been repressed and which may account for his behavior to his parents in the present. The adolescent reacts to his parents not only as they are in his immediate present—the parent who supports him, with whom he may be argumentative, demanding or quarrelsome—but also in terms of the fantasied and remembered parent of his early formative years. The adolescent's reaction to his parents in the present is the out-

167

come of all the behavior which evolves from his relationship to his parents of the past, modified by defenses.

The parent of the adolescent may act differently from the way he did when the adolescent was a child. A parent may have beaten a young child or threatened severe physical punishment which created a certain adaptation, perhaps neurotic, in the child. When this child becomes an adolescent, the parent, instead of threatening or carrying out punishment, may now want to reason with the adolescent. But the adolescent will react to the parent in terms of the past.

While the parents may have changed, the change is usually gradual and not dramatic and it is therefore difficult for the adolescent to recognize that any change has taken place. If he feared his parents in the past, he may carry over his feelings so that he fears all adults without awareness that his fears are strange or inappropriate. The adolescent may also fear the counselor and consider that his behavior toward him is appropriate.

The adolescent sees his counselor as one more adult in the adult world and he thinks that the counselor must inevitably react the way other adults have reacted to him. He therefore will react as he does to other adults. In treatment adolescents do not so much relive the original trauma as continue to live it, since the situation persists into the present. For example, a boy who feels ambivalent toward his father and reacts to him with ambivalence is at times close and friendly with his male counselor and at other times hostile and withdrawn. He repeats toward him the behavior which exists in the present toward his father.

While the characteristic method of dealing with parents persists, childhood memories are usually repressed especially in early and middle adolescence. Adolescents do not ordinarily talk much about what happened before the adolescent period and even when they do it is without the meaning and intensity of affect which adults show when they uncover childhood memories. Occasionally the children of introspective or psychologizing parents may have recall of chidlhood memories but they use their memories exploitively rather than for understanding and this type of defensive recall can complicate rather than aid treatment. Older adolescents have a greater interest in remembering and rediscovering their childhood and in treatment can orient themselves in this direction.

Adolescents handle infantile traumas in various ways. Some adolescents continue to behave in a manner determined by a trauma of the past; but at the same time that the behavior aroused by the trauma continues overtly in the present, the young adolescents are not interested in reviving the memory of the past trauma. Even when a difficulty arises out of infantile trauma, the experience is not actually in the past. It continues into the present. The adolescent is unwilling to recall the original episodes because his behavior does not seem to him to be irrelevant to the present.

Apart from the actual repression of early memories, young adolescents do not want to talk about their childhood in treatment because they are chronologicaly close to it and do not have the distance necessary to be comfortable in reliving the past. Unwillingness is added to the repression. If the affects are revived, they may be too intense for the adolescent to tolerate.

Moreover, younger adolescents continue to use some of their latency defenses; they hold back on feeling more than do older adolescents and adults. Young adolescents express their feelings to their parents in their behavior, although they may withhold unacceptable feelings and fantasies.

Life experience gives an adult defenses to use in dealing with his feelings, and he can be less fearful when he revives old feelings. An adolescent has just achieved some measure of maturity and is struggling desperately to maintain his new status through an excessive show of independence, rebellion or other adolescent manifestations. He is therefore more reluctant to give up any part of this rudimentary adulthood by returning even in memory to childhood experiences.

In general, then, the early adolescent deals with his counselor as he is currently dealing with his parents and the other important adults in his life. With his counselor, his teachers and other adults however, his fellings may not be quite as openly expressed as with his parents because most adolescents observe certain proprieties in situations outside their own homes. But in whatever way the adolescent behaves with his counselor, whether the behavior is more or less controlled than at home or whether it is a carryover of the way he currently acts with his parents, it is not a transference exclusively from the past. It is, more accurately, a repetition of the present situation with the parents. There are exceptions and occasionally an adolescent who is not afraid of his feelings may, in some instances, express feelings to his counselor which come from the past as well as the present.

Adolescents have a characteristic way of reacting to adults simply because they are adults. The adolescent is in a childhood role with a number of significant adults in his life, his parents, other relatives, teachers and employers. He has acquired a characteristic way of relating to grownups which he learned in early childhood and which continues into adolescence although modified to some degree. He has acquired an adaptive behavior to adults in general.

The adolescent may behave inappropriately in a manner which is repetitious not to the current situation only, but to situations either with his parents in the present or his parents as he viewed them in the past. This behavior seems appropriate to him and also to the adults around him. The adolescent does not consider his behavior needs to be examined or is a cause for concern because, living in it, he has no distance from which to observe himself objectively. The parents of the adolescent accept the behavior even when they do not like it; childish behavior in an adolescent is not regarded in the same way as if an adult began to act childish and parents usually do not see childish behavior as inappropriate to the adolescent's personality. Most parents do not understand the cause of the behavior and the references rooted in the past. Both the adolescent and his parents are embedded in a situation that neither sees as repetitious of the past.

Generally efforts to interpret present behavior as transference are rejected by adolescents. They are vitally involved with their problems of the present and see no need for relating them to the past. The conflict-laden aspects of the transference are difficult for young adults to endure.

The therapeutic relationship with adolescents depends so strongly on present gratification that they reject any discussion of negative elements in that relationship. They are fearful that they may lose the gratification the relationship provides if they have negative attitudes. The adolescent does not want to hear anything that will make his relationship to his counselor more distant or more professional.

There is, of course, ambivalence in the relationship with the counselor and the adolescent does have both positive and negative feelings. But if the counselor interprets the negative aspects of the relationship the adolescent is frightened that the counselor will see all of his "badness." Giving emphasis predominantly to the negative side of the ambivalence adds to that part of the adolescent's anxiety which makes him wish to withdraw from the therapeutic relationship. Persistence by the counselor on presenting negative aspects may lead to termination on the part of the adolescent. The positives must outweigh the negatives or the adolescent will not remain in treatment; he does not want to endure the pain of persistent negative affect toward his counselor.

Adolescents are conscious of negative feelings in the present toward their parents and counselor and will compare the counselor hostilely to a parent. "You're just like my father, always on my back." But this is not recognition of a transference reaction from the past. The adolescent feels his hostility is justified on the basis of present realities.

While an adolescent can tolerate less interpretation of the transference than adults, he feels freer to make comments on what he thinks is the counselor's emotional reaction to him. He is still consciously preoccupied with the nature of his parents' behavior in the present and therefore is alert to seeing others behave toward him as his parents do. Therapeutic effort to show an adolescent that this is a transference manifestation will usually bring a negative reaction. The adolescent has no insight into his own role. Rather he sees the counselor's attitude as a realistic replica of his parents', not a misconception on his own part.

It is possible, and it is important therapeutically, to make interpretations of transference in relation to the displacement of behavior from a parent to another person, as for instance a teacher. The adolescent does not consciously get insight or perceive the correctness of the transference interpretation, but he is affected by interpretations even though he will not directly acknowledge that he accepts them. Stating the interpretation may, without his verbal acceptance, bring about a change in the adolescent's behavior.

Following a significant interview, an adolescent may have a strong reaction to a teacher; subsequently in treatment he reports what happened with the teacher. The counselor knows the adolescent is unconsciously talking about his reactions to him. In treatment the counselor discusses the way the adolescent acted with his teacher. It is possible to discuss actual behavior reported by the adolescent and to interpret it dynamically. He will accept that, but he will not readily accept interpretations of his behavior as displacement of feelings about his counselor. The unwillingness of the adolescent to accept interpretations about the nature of the relationship between himself and his counselor is a consequence of the importance of the relationship, his reluctance to consider disturbing affect and his sensitivity to having these feelings brought into the open.

In the course of prolonged treatment the older adolescent will come to recognize many of his reactions to his counselor as transference from his parents, past and present. Under those circumstances, the counselor deals with them interpretively. Whenever the adolescent recognizes transference reactions the counselor acknowledges them. When transference interferes with the continuation of treatment it must be interpreted even though the adolescent may be resistant.

In summary, the specific difference in transference manifestations in adolescents as distinct from adults is that the adolescent's parents are still present and extremely significant in his psychological life. The adolescent does not generally think of his behavior toward his parents as neurotic or inappropriate because there is a conscious continuity of the attitude toward the parents. While transference is repetition in the present of feelings, attitudes and behavior from the past, it is not a simple repetition. Adolescents have a mixed reaction to their parents on the basis of their reaction to them in the past. The mixture is caused by the infantilism in the adolescent, and the reality of the present and may range from a predominantly realistic reaction by the adolescent to a predominantly transference reaction in which the current attitudes and behavior of the parent plays only a small part. The counselor must recognize this double nature of the transference which takes place toward him. With an adolescent the counselor makes the transference conscious only when it is absolutely necessary in order to continue treatment.

A number of transference factors make it advisable for adolescents usually to be treated by counselors of the same sex as their own. Most adolescents are more comfortable with persons of their own sex because they are preoccupied with their own newly discovered sexual feelings about which they may be in conflict. Communication with a counselor of the opposite sex would be more difficult for most adolescents. Also, adolescents are searching for their own identity and it is easier to find such an identity with a counselor of the same sex.

There are certain adolescents for whom counselors of the same sex are definitely indicated.

Sexually acting-out adolescents or those whose defensive structure is such that they have a tendency to over-sexualize relationships require a counselor of the same sex.

Young adolescent boys need identification with a male counselor. Because infantile male adolescents will usually relate well to a woman, the mistake is frequently made of assuming that a woman will meet their therapeutic needs. But the ego ideal issues, including the ideal of masculinity, makes a male counselor essential. The masculinization of the young boy is so important that it overrides other therapeutic considerations. Boys are rarely as sure of their masculinity as girls are about their femininity; girls are more certain of their sexual identity because males must shift the original identification from their mothers. The treatment goal for infantile boys is to help them to mature independence even though a large part of the treatment techniques, especially at the outset, is based on a giving relationship. A male counselor can give to an adolescent boy without fostering a deep dependent regression or undue and prolonged dependency. A woman counselor would need to frustrate the dependency in order to encourage growth and this initial frustration would make the therapeutic task more difficult.

In spite of the probable attendant difficulties it is more culturally acceptable for an adolescent girl to develop sexual feelings about an older male. But it would be very difficult for an adolescent boy to handle his problems around sexuality with a woman counselor. Cultural as well as technical issues make it more difficult for a woman to treat most adolescent boys.

In some individual instances however a counselor of the opposite sex may have therapeutic value.

A girl whose anxieties about her mother are so strong that she is unable to relate to any woman might profit from a male counselor even in the face of the possibility that erotic feelings may develop in the relationship. A girl whose problem does not primarily involve fear of her mother, but who needs help in working through inhibitions against interest in males might gain from the experience of establishing a relationship with a male counselor. However, when fear of the mother is an important issue, a female counselor is indicated in order to allow the fear to emerge and be worked out through a benign relationship with a woman. Where a combination of factors exist, transfer to a male counselor might be indicated at a point when the adolescent girl has resolved some of the anxieties with a female counselor.

Girls may gain from relationship with a male counselor when they defend themselves against sexuality because of an apathetic father, or a father who is not interested in them, or a father who was prohibitive sexually.

A corrective emotional experience may be provided by a male counselor for a girl who lost her father early in life and who has had no adequate male substitute figure.

A dependent young adolescent boy who has suffered actual deprivation of a mother figure, or who has had a rejecting hostile mother might be helped by providing him with a benign female counselor. However, the dependency component would have to be weighed carefully against the issue of sexual identity and conflict.

A boy in great conflict with his father on an overt behavioral level, and who cannot get along with other males might profitably use a woman counselor. A boy might have a specific kind of conflict with his mother that could only be worked through in a relationship with a woman counselor. An example of this is anxiety about positive feelings for the mother, where the father was not the source of the anxiety. A woman counselor could in such an instance provide a corrective emotional experience by allowing the boy's positive feelings about women to develop.

A counselor of the opposite sex is probably advisable for an adolescent where there are indications that strong homosexual attachment to the counselor might develop which creates unmanageable treatment problems. If homosexual attachment becomes evident in the course of treatment, transfer to another counselor might be indicated if it cannot be worked through.

Adolescents who express very strong preference for a counselor of the opposite sex should be allowed to follow their stated preference because otherwise they might be difficult to engage in treatment.

Older adolescents, as they approach the beginnings of young adulthood, may be considered as adults with the choice of counselor based on individual dynamics and preferences.

Countertransference is inappropriate behavior and feelings in the counselor aroused by the individual he is treating. The counselor's behavior, neurotic or non-neurotic, is determined by his own psychodynamics. But the adolescent in treatment, because of what he is, or what he says or does, may evoke personal reaction in the counselor.

Not everything a counselor does in the session and not all of his own feelings are countertransference reactions. In the treatment of adolescents it is necessary to separate the deliberate therapeutic activities from the counselor's spontaneous personal reactions. Treatment with adolescents calls for a wide range of helping efforts; the adolescent's counselor on many occasions takes an active role; he instructs, advises, and sometimes intervenes with parental or community figures. Attitude demonstrations are a therapeutic necessity with adolescents;

they are deliberate professional activities, appearing as spontaneous reactions, and should not be confused with countertransference.

Many other issues besides the adolescent's personality impinge on the counselor; he may be physically or psychologically fatigued; he may have had a difficult or harassing interview immediately preceding the present one. These factors contribute to the way the counselor feels at a particular moment although they may not relate to the individual he is seeing at the moment.

The counselor must be aware of his own affect and behavior, whether it has been aroused by the individual he is treating or by other factors, although he cannot always be completely conscious of his own reactions. He must scrutinize himself as much as he can without making the scrutiny itself a countertransference defense, an isolating technique which precludes being alert to the adolescent. A counselor must have the capacity to notice his own behavior and feelings, and the self-observation in itself is of value. It is useful to stand back from whatever emotional state he may be in and consider how his own reaction is affecting the treatment of any particular adolescent. Charlotte Towle has summed this up succinctly. "Professional maturation is marked by the point where self consciousness gives way to consciousness of self."

If the counselor can verbalize to himself what is going on within himself, it is easier to control his reactions and not yield to whatever countertransference may be aroused by the adolescent. The self-observation in itself tones down the intensity of his own feelings. The adolescent may sense the counselor's conflicts and act in a way to exacerbate them. Knowing this makes it easier for the counselor to control his own reactions. The counselor's own superego and ego ideal do not allow him to act out his own conflict on the adolescent he is treating. Once the counselor has observed and verbalized to himself to what he is reacting, he is in the process of acquiring self-control. Because he controls himself in relation to the adolescent the counselor appeases his own superego and feels better.

The adolescent is not responsible for the counselor's affect states; he only touches off feelings based on the counselor's pre-existing dynamics. The counselor will become aware that a negative reaction to a given adolescent is merely his own way of discharging his own affects aroused by that particular situation. The counselor who makes such self-observation may gain personal insights. But even without insights, observation of the self will stave off negative affects so that they are not discharged on the adolescent.

This self-scrutiny is less difficult if something specific in connection with the adolescent arouses a state in the counselor different from what was previously taking place. If a session was going well and suddenly the counselor finds himself irritated, he should be able to grasp what specifically has happened to arouse this deviant state.

When the counselor recognizes his own feelings, his particular affect state of the moment, whether it is fatigue, or physical discomfort, disouragement or lack of investment in the adolescent may be lessened to some extent, so that he is better able to go on in a therapeutic and positive way.

Chronic attitudes toward certain adolescents are less likely to be observed by the counselor because such attitudes are preconscious. These attitudes may be positive or negative; if they are positive, they are of minor concern. Positive feelings on the part of the counselor are good for the treatment of the adolescent. Even if the positive feeling is neurotically based it is possible to maintain a professional attitude by giving thought to the feelings.

In the treatment of adolescents the more frequent positive attitudes which occur are maternal, paternal and protective feelings. Frequently there is identification with the adolescent and his problems. The adolescent usually profits from such positive feelings on the part of his counselor, especially in the beginning of treatment. Most adolescents respond with great pleasure to the feeling that the counselor likes them. Here too, though, the counselor must be aware of his own positive feelings and not let them interfere with the techniques necessary to help the adolescent. Without such awarenes he might, for example, hold an adolescent in treatment longer than is necessary because the warm positive interaction makes professional life gratifying.

The fundamental necessity of every therapeutic relationship with an adolescent is that the counselor's feelings be predominantly of a benign nature. It is therefore essential to be particularly observant of negative feelings. The positive feelings do not have to be love. Empathy, understanding, identification in whole or part with the adolescent make it possible to feel positively inclined toward the adolescent, even with one whose way of life may be incompatible with the counselor's. Within the context of a professional relationship these reactions help him to feel rapport, or establish an essentially positive attitude. Occasional negative feelings do not ruin the relationship if the overall attitude is a positive one.

Every adolescent has many different qualities and the counselor tries to find some aspect that he can like or become interested in, if only as an intellectual challenge. For example, an understanding counselor knows that it is difficult for anyone to like some anal characters because their defensive structure keeps them from displaying any liking for others. He knows that this kind of adolescent must not allow any positive feelings toward the counselor or anyone else, for fear of rejection or frustration. He will expect the adolescent to be angry and his awareness will keep him from responding with angry counterfeelings. If the anal adolescent has repressed his anger he will show only coldness and distance, with repetitive behavior and attitudes designed to frustrate the counselor. But the counselor realizes that the adolescent cannot feel warmth because that implies an expectation of warmth in return and his unhappy experience has led him to feel no positive response will be forth-coming. The counselor may not be able to like this adolescent immediately but his understanding may create sympathy for the unhappy, cold, unfeeling adolescent. When the counselor is aware of his negative feelings toward this kind of adolescent he can use his awareness for therapeutic purposes.

Dependency is a common need of adolescents which occa-sionally may arouse negative countertransference. Dependent adolescents who feel that they have never been sufficiently loved or have never been given to with sufficient gratification seem determined to prove that they cannot be gratified. They are frustrating to treat because they seem insatiable. There are many such adolescents and it is important to be conscious of the feel-ings they arouse. The counselor may manage his own reactions by an internal verbalization of the situation such as: "Here is a typical dependent adolescent. He feels that his parents did nothing for him, and nobody else is going to do anything for him. He is out to prove that I can't help him." The advantage of being aware of the countertransference is that it allows the counselor to determine what specifically in the dependency arouses his negative response. Then, perhaps the counselor can tell the adolescent he has a special problem which the counselor can feel; he may be able to show the adolescent that his own demanding behavior arouses negative or hostile reactions. He can ask the adolescent to consider whether his current trouble stems actually from the fact that his parents do not give him enough or do enough for him or whether part of the problem is the adolescent's insatiable demands which bring on negative responses.

When actual deprivation of early dependent gratifications has occurred, some individuals become resigned and give up the idea of being loved, while others become aggressive, demanding and angrily grab at any possibility for gratification. Such adolescents arouse negative countertransference reactions and yet the de-manding adolescent offers good prognosis for treatment because he will grasp at a giving relationship. The adolescents who have given up are less amenable to treatment because relationships may no longer have hopeful meaning for them.

But bolstered by awareness of his own countertransference, the counselor should not be too quick to jump to the conclusion that any adolescent is not treatable. Many acting-out adolescents are denying feelings of loss and of unlovableness by their activities and by rebellion against their own superegos. Once the underlying depressed affect is detected, the counselor's attitude warms and he can reach out to such an adolescent. The continuation or termination of any treatment should depend on the therapeutic problems rather than on countertransference reaction.

If a counselor finds that his attitude toward an adolescent is predominantly negative he should allow himself time to try to work out his own feelings. If the negative feelings persist, it is in the interest of the adolescent to effect transfer to another counselor.

Because of the state of the adolescent ego, special countertransference problems are aroused by adolescents in treatment. Adults manage their own lives, even when they are in treatment. But adolescents sometimes need active help. When the adolescent is in some reality difficulty counselors have a tendency to become aroused. They feel the need to intervene because of the ego deficiencies and inexperience and also because of the permanent effect some unwise or precipitate actions may have on the adolescent's life. An adolescent may reveal to his counselor that he is planning to quit school or run away from home. The counselor immediately reacts with concern about the consequences and this concern will motivate activities on the counselor's part other than interrogation or interpretation. Consciously, counselors want to deter acting out. But unconsciously the counselor may have other attitudes and feelings, perhaps punitive or prohibitive feelings about the particular form of acting out.

Adolescents will pick up these feelings and accuse the counselor of thinking of him as bad, of interfering or of acting like a bad parent. The focus of the counselor should always be what is best for a particular adolescent at that point in time. When a counselor is impelled to intervene actively he should do so only after consideration of his own emotional reactions. A counselor who is calm is more effective than one who is carried away by the crisis nature of a situation.

The counselor cannot be neutral about certain kinds of behavior which involve harmful consequences to the adolescent or to others. He must present the consequences of such behavior to the adolescent and indicate his own concern, based on his genuine interest in the adolescent. The adolescent may react as if the counselor were moralizing, he may resent what the counselor says, but when his ultimate welfare is jeopardized the counselor must risk the possibility of negative or hostile reaction from the adolescent. Adults may choose their own standards of values and take the responsibility for their own behavior. Adolescents are not yet ready for this responsibility and the counselor who treats adolescents must be concerned with their ego ideals and superego values.

It is possible for a counselor to discover in every adolescent traits of character with which his affective responses are empathic, or some aspect of the individual with which he can identify, or, the problem itself can become engrossing. When he is able to find something within the adolescent that he can respond to positively, the counselor is relieved of hopeless feelings, or the frustration of working without immediate result. Treatment becomes a cheerless and ungratifying task without the satisfactions that come from seeing beneficial results. Since there cannot always be therapeutic succcess, the counselor must find gratifications in learning from experience and in increasing refinement of his awareness of the helping process.

When a counselor has negative feelings about an individual adolescent he must always ask himself why. The professional superego and ego ideal of the counselor will help him to relate to adolescents that he would not otherwise like. The counselor who does not have this kind of professional orientation cannot work with adolescents because he will not be able to involve different kinds of adolescents in a therapeutic relationship.

# 11

# The Parents of Adolescents in Treatment

ADOLESCENCE IS AN AGE of anxiety for parents as well as for the adolescent. Even parents of normal adolescents often feel bewildered, attacked, rebelled against, insecure in their authority, worried about the present and fearful of the future. They are affected by the widespread popular knowledge that adolescence is a difficult age, and they are alarmed by the publicity about the prevalence of delinquency and the many dangers and threats to their own children.

During the relative passivity of the latency phase they have been lulled into composure which they do not want to see disturbed. However much they prepare themselves for anticipated trouble, adolescence hits with a sharp emotional impact. The inner turmoil which adolescents undergo spills over into mutually troubled interactions. Although they may recognize that the adolescent growth process is the cause, parents need patience, fortitude, strength and humor to live calmly through upsets of the accustomed family balance.

One phase or another of his child's development may be difficult for any parent to integrate; which phase becomes conflict-laden depends on the individual history of the parent's own development. But most parents adapt themselves to the image they form of what their child is like during the early years. The sudden onset of adolescence often disrupts this image for the parents before they can adjust to the rapidly changing personality of their child. Counselors repeatedly hear the complaint from adolescents, "They treat me like a baby" and from parents, "He's acting too big for his britches." These complaints coincide with the actual in-between phase of the adolescent personality development which makes difficulty for parents in deciding how much independence the adolescent should be allowed.

Some parents cling to the childhood image of the adolescent for fear of accepting their own aging. Not uncommonly, mothers are ambivalent, somewhat jealous of the beauty of a budding daughter with all its implications. Parents may prefer to continue thinking of the adolescent as a child out of fears about the possibility of his yielding to sexual impulse. Sexuality is almost universally a conflict and parents of adolescents almost without exception are concerned about promiscuity, pregnancy, and premature marriage, especially for daughters. The concern may lead to excessive controls on the one hand, or reactive over-permissiveness on the other. It is not easy for any parent to avoid the extremes.

To see a previously dependent child, whose very dependency made him manageable, become independent is often painful for the parent. The sudden lack of communication, the secretiveness, the shift from home-centered life to unknown and frequently feared outside bases is disheartening or saddening for parents, if not irritating and provoking. Concerned parents become anxious about not knowing the adolescent's whereabouts, friends, activities and purposes. But lack of concern is not a satisfactory answer; an indifferent parent probably has least control over the behavior of his adolescent child.

The great discomfort for the parent lies in facing his own adolescent anxieties once again as they are reawakened within himself by his adolescent child. Gradually, during his own adolescent years, the parent achieved character synthesis through emotional struggle and compromise. When he became a young adult he found resolution of conflict and a measure of stability and by the time he became a parent his own character had become relatively settled. His attitudes, values and patterns of behavior became predictable and stable. With distress, therefore, the parent finds that the adolescence of his child brings to the surface again his own adolescent struggles. The adolescent may touch off in his parents old conflicts of being unloved, rejected. There may be a reawakened flaring of oedipal wishes in the parents, intensification of rivalries and competitiveness and revival of aggressive and sexual fears. All the issues the parents had settled somehow or somewhat for themselves are now stirred up again.

Many of the common difficulties between parents and adolescents about hair or dress styles, social behavior, study or work habits are the outer manifestations of the unconscious conflict about the adolescent's disruption of the adult status quo the parents had painfully achieved.

The adolescent's attempts at separation and emancipation will start reverberations which go back to his first years of life. The history may reveal doubts and fears in the mother when the child began to walk and could move away from her, difficulties when the child began school, or at the transition from elementary to high school. These normally are stress periods, for all parents; but for the parents of the troubled child the stresses increase. The parents will express themes of fear of separation, fear of losing the child, fear of not being needed. These parents are also more conscious of their own aging, their loss of youth and vigor. The adolescent's growth into young adulthood is viewed as all loss with no compensations because it may also be seen as loss of control and an inner fear that they have given nothing to their child, that he internalized nothing of them, and therefore, with his new freedom, he will do nothing well and will get into serious difficulties.

Parents look on adolescence as their last chance to correct ego weakness. The proximity to adulthood and the imminence of future-shaping decisions force parents to force their adolescent children; weaknesses are not tolerated as they had been before. If they have invested themselves deeply in their child, the parents must now have other emotional and social absorptions which make change endurable. The adolescent should not be, nor should he remain, the exclusive center of their lives.

The parents may feel the adolescent is a disappointment to them, not living up to their expectations. They sometimes fear he will fall short of what they wanted, or in some instances the fear is that he will exceed and outstrip them, making them feel inferior, ashamed and unwanted. They feel certain that without strong parental intervention their adolescent will not survive this difficult phase unscathed, will not be able to pull back from the brink of danger.

The adolescent's potential for sexual acting-out is frightening, and adolescent physical changes and growth are not welcomed as were the stages in growth of the young child. The adolescent reflects back to the parents what they most fear in themselves. The re-emergence of childhood problems, common in adolescence, which the parents thought were resolved, creates alarm and anxiety which only adds to the family upset.

Not all parents react uncomfortably to the adolescence of their children. Counselors see adolescents and parents who have problems and therefore inevitably emphasize the problem areas of parent-adolescent relationships. There are parents who can enjoy the adolescent development, who stand as bulwarks and guides for the adolescent struggles, and who grow with their children.

When an adolescent needs treatment because of social or emotional problems, his parents, who are inextricably involved in his life, should have an important part in the total therapeutic plan.

The counselor must appreciate that seeking treatment for an adolescent child is a painful experience for most parents. It represents a confession of failure in their own roles as competent successful parents. They approach the counselor anxiously, guiltily, hostilely or suspiciously. Out of these feelings competition with the counselor frequently arises, stimulating both conscious and unconscious antagonisms. If the counselor is not able to appreciate the position in which the parents find themselves, lack of this understanding may be sufficiently disturbing to the parents so that they refuse to involve themselves in the treatment plan or terminate treatment of the adolescent prematurely.

The natural tendency of a counselor to empathize with the adolescent he is treating must not cause him to forget that the parents, too, have their own needs, feelings and attitudes; their personalities are the outcome of their own life experiences, happy and unhappy, independent of their children, although interwoven with them. Counselors must remember that parents too had parents who made mistakes; but most parents, short of extreme pathology, do the best job of child rearing they are able to do under the circumstances.

The counselor should be prepared to give parents understanding of the adolescent process generally, and specifically as it applies to their own child. Often the parent's bewilderment is eased when he hears that bewilderment itself is to be expected. Parents are less anxious if they realize that the adolescent unpredictabilities are known, if not totally understandable, phenomena. To know, and to predict, that the adolescent will be unpredictable, frequently changes parental anger to amused annoyance and can quiet distressful household situations.

It is important for the parent to be told that by the time a child reaches adolescence, certain patterns of behavior and attitudes are already well-established and internalized and that these patterns may persist in the adolescent no matter what the parent does in the present. This understanding helps the parent realize that the adolescent needs help for himself in order to resolve or dilute these well entrenched patterns and helps to clarify and interpret the purposes of treatment.

Often the immediate reason for seeking treatment for an adolescent is a crisis situation. A court may offer probation if treatment is instituted; a school may defer expulsion on the same basis. The parents of these adolescents may see treatment as forced upon them, community pressure overriding their own natural functions as parents. Even when no outside source precipitates the request for treatment, there has usually been some critical drawing to a head of a family situation that may have been festering over a long period and which the parents recognize as beyond their capacity to handle or control. In these instances, too, the parents will feel shame at their own incapacity, a sense of defeat and helplessness in the face of problems and anxiety.

The counselor should meet troubled parents with benign expectations. Few parents are consciously or totally rejecting, few are openly hostile to their children. Most parents want to be good parents. The counselor will use this wish to be good parents as the motivation for involving them in the treatment. They can approach treatment for themselves with the hope that they will become better parents. The counselor must start out with the assumption that the parents are adequate adults who have managed their children in the best way they could, and who need help with a situation that has no quick and easy solution. Censure or an attitude of superiority defeats the therapeutic goal of offering the parent a share in a partnership of parent, adolescent and counselor all working together to effect beneficial changes.

In T. S. Eliot's *The Cocktail Party* the psychiatrist says, "Before I treat a patient, I need to know a good deal more about him than the patient himself can tell me. Indeed it is often the case that my patients are only pieces of a total situation which I have to resolve. The single patient who is ill by himself is rather the exception."

This statement is especially true of the adolescent. The counselor needs to have as much information about an adolescent as it is possible to obtain. Much of this information the adolescent himself cannot give. There are also realistic factors which make seeing the parents an obvious necessity: parental consent is needed for treatment; the parent needs to discuss fees, if fees are to be paid, and assume responsibility for payment; the already damaged parental authority needs to be restored; parents need to be oriented to the therapeutic process, to what they can expect from it and what the counselor will expect of them; their preoccupation with the source of referral, school, court or other person, should be diverted to the present situation; and they should be helped to prepare the adolescent for his first meeting with the counselor.

The nature of the relationship which is established with the parents is one of the strong determining factors in whether or not an adolescent continues in treatment.

In the initial contact with the parents the counselor has two main objectives. The first is to get their understanding and to create as favorable an attitude as is possible toward the treatment of their adolescent child. The second is to assess the potential of the parents for moving into a treatment relationship simultaneously with the adolescent so that they can be helped to modify those aspects of their relationship to their child which have hampered growth. In a dynamic process both of these objectives are fused and cannot be arbitrarily isolated. The accomplishment of these objectives, however, is not a simple task. The level of anxiety in the parents on initial contact is high, and so is the level of defensiveness.

When the referral is at the instigation of outside sources, such as the school or a court, the parents are often preoccupied with defending themselves with elaborate rationalizations of their actions as parents. They may be angry because of injustices, mishandling of their adolescent on the part of outside agencies, and misunderstanding.

Some parents are preoccupied with angry complaints about their adolescent. They also strongly defend their own actions and protect themselves with rationalizations. Typically these parents tell of having tried every technique from bribery to punishment in an effort to resolve the problems.

Only rarely is a parent totally sympathetic to the adolescent's problems or making an effort to understand as they might with small children. Parents of adolescents are angry, they feel attacked and with justification, because adolescents almost universally do attack their parents. The adolescent is especially adept at sensing and exacerbating the most vulnerable aspects of the parents' personality and behavior. Parents worry about their lack of influence over their adolescent, again with justification. But the feeling is sharply accentuated when there is continuous trouble and repeated failure.

Often they seem desperate and press for immediate action because they have the feeling that time is running out. Parents can be more relaxed with small children, who, they believe, will grow out of any particularly difficult phase. The behavior of adolescents threatens parents because it involves actual or potential conflict with the environment. The adolescent has the physical and emotional capacity to act out or to threaten such acting out. He can rebel vociferously, in school and at home.

Parents of small children readily give detailed developmental history and are receptive to interpretation of its importance. Parents of adolescents often are impatient with this procedure and will not accept or cannot understand any relationship with the present problem. They are, however, quite ready to discuss the precipitation and development of the current problem.

Ideally, to provide the climate in which treatment with the adolescent can be most successful, parents should be willing to keep regular appointments with the counselor, work hard on understanding the nature of the problem that confronts them and their adolescent, and modify those aspects of the environment that are disabling. They should be prepared to investigate the emotional conflicts that have played a part in the adolescent's troubles. And they should not interfere with the treatment of the adolescent.

Some parents can enter this kind of therapeutic partnership quickly but they are few in number. More prevalent are attitudes such as, "We are willing for Johnny to come to see you. Take him, teach him to respect his parents and his teachers, and to get better grades; tell him to stop going with bad boys and girls. But leave us out of it." Many parents are concerned with their own situation and not the adolescent's. "Look at all the trouble he has caused me" is much more common than "He is unhappy and I hope you can help him."

Counselors react to such statements from parents; the parents are viewed as resistant and ready to dump their own responsibility on to the counselor; treatment is regarded as a poor risk. Such parents may be poor risks but the counselor's attitude toward them must be carefully examined. He must remember that the parents have problems; that they have already experienced a barrage of criticism. The counselor is inclined to be less sympathetic to the adults than to the adolescent in intrafamily difficulties, but he must be sensitive to their hurt, disappointment and shame. Hopelessness and confusion are the predominant attitudes of such parents. The image of themselves as parents with control and authority over their homes and family, is substantially damaged and they experience a sense of failure, a loss of status and prestige. They may react with anger, denial, projection, guilt and depression, in accordance with their own individual character structures. They may strain the counselor's capacity to be tolerant and accepting but patience and understanding are what they need.

The counselor's first meeting with the parents is oriented around the presenting problem of the adolescent, its dimensions and ramifications, time of onset, precipitating factors, the areas of adjustment and maladjustment, the parental efforts to handle the problems and the adolescent's reactions to these efforts. The counselor asks for information about the adolescent's interests and activities, the kinds of adults he likes and dislikes and the basis for these feelings. With these starting points the parents are led into as much diagnostic information as they are ready or able to give. The approach is flexible; the counselor does not press for developmental history if the parents are resistant. Such information can always be obtained later and more appropriately in relation to questions or situations that develop in the ongoing treatment.

The parents want to discuss the immediate problem which led them to come for treatment for their adolescent; it is the current situation which troubles them. To obtain more general history, the parents have to move from their preoccupation with the immediate situation. The counselor's questions about onset of the difficulty provides opportunity for moving to the past. When a child has been a consistent source of conflict with this parents, in school, or elsewhere in his environment, parents can be taken back to the first months of infancy to trace the development of the pervasive trouble. With a child who has suddenly changed and is currently involved in an acute situation, the counselor tells the parents that he needs to understand what the child was like earlier in order to comprehend the extent of the change. In either case, with adolescents, unlike younger children, parents will need a gradual process of working back since they ordinarily do not see the reasons for giving a straight chronological developmental history.

The initial contacts with the parents consist of a broad survey of the present problems with as much genetic information as the parents are ready to give, and with as much affect as the skill of the counselor can elicit.

Mothers are more readily available than fathers and are therefore more easily involved in treatment, but it is also important for the father to be interviewed, and to attempt to involve him in treatment. The counselor needs to know the attitude of each parent toward the treatment, not only to understand the viewpoint of each parent but also to emphasize the importance of both parents; from each parent a picture of the family is obtained which fits together into a more complete whole than either parent alone could give. The counselor should never fall into the trap of accepting one parent's picture of the other. For example, it is not uncommon for mothers to depict the father as an insignificant factor in the adolescent's problems or as an unimportant part of the family. But when it is impossible to involve the father in treatment the counselor may have to continue with the mother alone.

Parents have difficulty in interpreting treatment to their adolescent. However carefully the counselor structures with the parent ways in which he might introduce the adolescent to treatment, the parent's own unconscious needs determine his method of presentation. The adolescent then adds his own fantasies and distortions. The parental explanations will carry all the coloring of the disturbed parent-child relationship. The adolescent who is underachieving in school may be given an interpretation of treatment which he can readily confuse with tutoring service; an adolescent who is in trouble in his environment may be led to believe that he is sentenced to see an official somewhat like a probation officer. Even the most sophisticated parents who understand what is involved in treatment may give an interpretation which frightens the adolescent into doubts about his sanity (a real and present question with many adolescents in any case). The counselor therefore works out with the parents an approach to the adolescent that seems most comfortable to them and then anticipates that distortions will occur. The important task for the parents is to get the adolescent to appear when an appointment is scheduled for him.

Parents are apprehensive about the process of treatment itself, which is an unknown to most people. It requires personal involvement and the expenditure of time and money. Frequently parents resent the fact that outsiders are entering into their affairs; they are sure that all the negatives in the family situation and relationships will be brought to light; they may equate psychological illness with badness. These feelings are strengthened by the popular notion that there are no delinquent children, only delinquent parents. Parents will frequently distort information about the problem or the family situation in order to create a more favorable impression. But counselors must try to convey that parents and children are interrelated personalities, each with his own constitutional factors, each reacting uniquely, and each shaped by his personal life history. Whatever the initial causes of the difficulty, problems of adolescents and their parents become interactional. This concept can be reassuring to parents.

Parents also need reassurance that they have acted wisely about seeking help for their adolescent; that they are doing something constructive about their problems. The purpose of this is not only to alleviate anxiety, but to enable the exploratory process to move on as smoothly as possible. Premature general reassurance should be avoided since this shuts out further exploration.

The counselor should convey to parents that he is interested in the parents' as well as the adolescent's problems. He lets them know that he is experienced with their particular kind of difficulty. The counselor cannot promise specific improvement, for example, he cannot promise improvement in school grades, but he can realistically hold out hope based on having been helpful in similar situations.

Parents should be encouraged to ask questions and the counselor should answer the questions honestly and with respect while trying to recognize what is behind the questions. Some are cover-ups for anxiety rather than a request for information, but there need not be a hidden motive behind every question. The counselor, in his first contact with the parent, wants the parent to learn who he is, how he works and why; he conveys an attitude of expertness, of benign authority, of non-defensiveness, and of acceptance of the parent's right to think, feel, and say whatever he wishes.

No matter how well-defended the parent may be, the counselor recognizes that his narcissism is wounded by the failures implicit in his child's need for treatment. The parent can better accept his role in the helping process if he gets some immediate narcissistic gratification. The counselor will emphasize the helpfulness of the parent's discussion of problems and attitudes. He will let the parent know that he realizes how important his adolescent child is to him, and that the adolescent's difficulties are making the parent unhappy. He indicates as one of the aims of treatment more comfort and less trouble in the life of the parent.

Sometimes parents put pressure on the counselor for immediate advice, but he should withstand this pressure, explaining to the parent that time is needed to understand the problems. This establishes the counselor as an expert who is not given to easy solutions or pat formulae and who functions on a sound basis. Premature advice-giving may set up expectations of easy answers which are neither practical nor tenable. At the outset the counselor really does not know what advice would be appropriate or the parent's capacity to follow suggestions.

Advice is sometimes given to parents as part of the treatment of an adolescent, but within the context of the treatment relationship. If the parent can give good descriptions of the situation and if the counselor has had time to understand the adolescent, some details of parental handling may be formulated. To avoid disappointment, however, the parent should be told that the suggested techniques may not work. But, often, dramatic improvements occur from a change in overt tactics.

If the parent has sincere motivation to improve his management of the adolescent, even intellectual insight into the dynamic interaction with the adolescent will help, provided the insight is acceptable. For example, a father who has been competing with his son out of unconscious sibling rivalry feelings, may be able to recognize on an intellectual level that he has been reacting neurotically to the adolescent's behavior. With no basic change in his own internal dynamics, he may be able to grit his emotional teeth and endure the adolescent behavior with less irritation than he did before.

The motivation for treatment of parents can best be evaluated not by verbalizations but by an evaluation of their character structure and in relation to the interaction beween counselor and parent. At the beginning it is the task of the counselor to determine how much contact the parents are willing to accept, rather than to analyze apparent resistances or to attempt to convince the parent that treatment will be helpful to him as well as to his adolescent. The counselor will settle for what he can get realistically. For example, a parent who quite clearly indicates that he does not wish to involve himself in treatment may be willing to come for four or five interviews on the basis of giving history and information. A parent who is uncertain about his desire to engage himself may be receptive to a limited trial period. The adolescent's treatment will benefit from treatment of the parent but an adolescent may be helped even if his parents refuse any involvement. The minimum requirement from the parent is consent for the adolescent's treatment. But parents can move far beyond their initial readiness, and few parents will be content with an attitude of total non-involvement toward the counselor's relationship with the adolescent.

It is useless to force parents by setting conditions. Parents who are desperate about their adolescent's difficulties will ostensibly agree to anything to initiate help for the adolescent. This is particularly true when treatment is offered as an alternative for some type of official action, such as suspension from school or even commitment to a disciplinary or correctional institution. Parents who have been pushed to agree to conditions without true motivation will have an inevitable reaction which eventually complicates the treatment relationships. Such parents feel they have been taken advantage of, or experience great guilt when they cannot fulfill the promises they made under pressure.

In addition, setting conditions, no matter how carefully done, inevitably involves the use of authority with parents whose authority has already been threatened by the adolescent and those community forces with which the adolescent has been in difficulty. Although the parents may have respect for authority they may also feel hostile to an extent that may cause them to withdraw their request for treatment for the adolescent; or, more subtly, their smoldering resentment may cause them to sabotage treatment. Similar reactions will result from premature efforts to penetrate their defenses, or overcome their resistances in order to obtain either information or compliance.

The prime goal initially with parents is to create as favorable an attitude as is possible toward the treatment of the adolescent. Any attitude is accepted from wholehearted parental cooperation down to little or none beyond permission to treat the adolescent.

At best, however, parents can be expected to be ambivalent in the beginning of contact and any agreements they may make about involving themselves in treatment must be considered as tentative. Their decision, ultimately, will be based, not so much on a conviction about the values of treatment as on a variety of other reasons. Hopefully, and ideally, they get an immediate feeling of trust and faith in the counselor; they may feel relief that the burden of the adolescent problem is being taken over, in whole or in part; they may be ready to abdicate in the expectation that the counselor can exercise control over the adolescent where they could not.

But whatever effect the counselor has upon them, they will retain the same attitudes they brought into the initial contact. With the parent, as with the adolescent, the counselor must look for the strengths in the midst of the pathology. He proceeds on the basis that the parents consciously wish for the improvement of their adolescents. Because they do wish for improvement, they will, within the limits of their own capacities, involve themselves in behalf of their adolescent.

How and to what extent the parents of an adolescent are involved with the adolescent's problems, and how much they should be involved with his treatment can only be determined through the diagnostic process. But the many complicated interactions, together with strong interests and concerns about their adolescents, indicate that some degree of parental involvement is essential. Adolescents are realistically dependent on their families at the same time that they are experiencing pressure to become integrated individuals, autonomous and self-directing. The parents' attitudes and feelings about realistic and psychological dependency and how they react to the adolescent's push toward separation from the parents require diagnostic evaluation and may call for treatment of the parent.

The kind of attitudes which seriously impede parents from living comfortably with their adolescent children may also impede therapeutic work with the adolescent. Overpermissiveness or overprotectiveness may be related to: overidentification with the adolescent's dependent or hostile wishes; overcompensation for parental rejecting and hostile feelings; a need to control the adolescent by keeping him dependent; or a need to identify with the adolescent's achievement. When an overpermissive attitude exists, effective parental relationship with the adolescent is blocked because the adolescent associates any limit setting with feelings of hostility rather than seeing it as helpful and realistic.

Parents may have competitive attitudes, related to rivalry with the adolescent as a sibling, or rivalry with him for achievement. A hostile and rejecting attitude is often associated with rivalry with the adolescent for dependency gratification or as a result of the adolescent's failure to meet the parent's own unresolved narcissistic needs. Parents may feel rivalrous with the counselor for the adolescent's affection and response.

The adolescent himself will not uncommonly create trouble in the parent-counselor relationship. The adolescent will sense if the parent resents the counselor or is competitive with him. Adolescents are quick to locate their parents' tender spots and irritate them; they have uncanny skill in sensing parental feelings. The father who feels inadequate in his role as a parent will not feel kindly toward a counselor whom his son describes as a better man or as one who knows more and understands better than the father. But if the father is involved in the helping process himself and can bring his feelings to his counselor, the parent may be kept from sabotaging the adolescent's treatment.

The task of helping a child renounce the infantile pleasures and the omnipotent longings and expectations is beyond the capacity of some parents. They maintain their own infantile longings and are enraged at the forced independence adulthood imposes on them, the requirements of being a parent, and the need to assist children gradually to give up infantile demands. When parental responsibility is deeply resented, the parents regard each developmental phase of growth, not only adolescence, as an arduous struggle. The demands projected on the adolescent, and the demands the adolescent projects on his parents, form part of the defensive facades and enter the treatment process. The counselor must tolerate the demands without anger or discouragement and without vacillating in his relationship to the mother, the father or the adolescent.

Adolescents often offer valid criticism of their parents but it is dangerous for the counselor who is treating the adolescent to over-identify with him and reject his parents. Despite his wish for autonomy, parents represent many positive security values for the adolescent and he fears his rejecting feelings will cause his parents to abandon him. If the counselor too readily supports the separation from the parents, in anxiety the adolescent reverts to greater dependency upon his parents to negate the temptation that seems too dangerous. Premature encouragement of emancipation from the parents in minor details also may mean encouragement to abandon everything the parents represent. Adolescents need secure new standards before they can safely abandon parental standards. Emancipation from the parents must take place and adolescents need to be supported in their efforts, but as Dr. Josselyn has pointed out the emancipation will be most constructively handled if it is encouraged to occur by evolution rather than by revolution.

While in some instances one counselor may work successfully with both the adolescent and his parents, more often separate counselors are indicated. Adolescents generally resent sharing their counselor and they also need to be assured of confidentiality. Should it be necessary to share or convey certain information to the parents, this should be discussed first with the adolescent.

There should be clear lines of communication between the adolescent's counselor and the parents' counselor. On certain occasions the parents may want direct contact, by phone or in person, with the adolescent's counselor and this should be permitted. Excessive interference or demands can be dealt with in the same way as any other problem in treatment.

At times of adolescent-parent crisis, the counselor may need to take the adolescent's position but this should be done for therapeutic purposes, with sufficient explanation to the parents, and not out of identification with the adolescent or out of hostility to the parent. Identification or hostility are not part of the treatment situation but are countertransference problems which need insight and control on the part of the counselor.

In his empathy with the adolescent the counselor must consciously guard against any feeling that parents are, by their very existence, the negative factors in the situation. It is possible to give fully of sympathy and understanding to an adolescent without depreciating the parent's role and without undermining the inherent parental dignity and authority either in the adolescent's or the counselor's thinking.

Upon occasion parents communicate information to the counselor which they do not wish the adolescent to know. This sometimes occurs in relation to family skeletons, secrets in the family background, and sometimes in relation to facts which directly pertain to the adolescent, such as adoption. When the counselor feels, after consideration of timing and the effect upon the adolescent, that the information should be given to the adolescent he will discuss this necessity with the parents.

There are occasions when to further treatment with an adolescent the counselor needs to intercede with the parents in concrete matters of parent-adolescent relationships, family rules and household practice. Many minor items can become the battleground on which serious emotional battles are fought; such things as household chores, dating hours, the use of the family car, allowances, the length of skirts or hair are frequent conflict areas. A counselor may need to work delicately with parents to persuade them to alter their rules without having them feel that they have been forced to abdicate their parental roles. The counselor will try to alter conflict-laden practices in order to show parents how to concede without losing parental authority.

Parents always need to be prepared for two major aspects of the treatment with adolescents: first, for no quick change, and secondly, for changes when they occur. In spite of careful orientation to what is involved in treatment many parents expect miraculous improvement. They become discouraged if no drastic change is seen in a short period of time and may then communicate this discouragement to the adolescent. Parental disapproval may center about the payment of fees, or show itself in an intensification of nagging, pressuring or an attitude of hopelessness which communicates itself to the adolescent.

In making sure that parents know that changes may not occur quickly it is necessary for the counselor to balance on a tight rope, never swaying to the point of indecisiveness where the parent feels that the counselor is no more competent than he is himself, and never becoming so positive or dogmatic that the parent feels his own authority is being undermined. The counselor cannot make promises of immediate improvement of the manifest behavior of the adolescent. He does not offer immediate concrete advice or panaceas, although many parents plead for a quick prescription, the equivalent of a massive injection of antibiotics. Yet the counselor must inspire confidence that he can be helpful, that he does not intend to usurp the parental role and that the treatment can be expected to be effective for parent and adolescent.

Parents are sometimes disturbed by the changes that do take place and may not immediately see them as desirable. They need help to understand the adolescent's considered steps toward emancipation or expressions of hostility previously feared and denied.

How the parents view the adolescent's problem, how they suffer or do not suffer with it, the specific issues which trouble them, and which of the adolescent's difficulties do not concern them, must be evaluated for treatment of the adolescent to be effective. If the parents are not involved in the treatment process knowledge of improvement when it occurs will need to be estimated from the clinical process. What the adolescent does on the outside, and what he does in relationship to his parents can only be guessed at, uncertainly. Also, how much undoing the parents may be engaged in as the adolescent resists the therapeutic efforts, is left to hazardous speculation. What goals the parents hold for their child, what they expect of him, what pressures they create, remain unknown, unless the adolescent has good capacity to perceive and articulate to the counselor. To ignore the motives and wishes of parents provides only a quicksand foundation on which to structure a treatment process.

There are some parents who are not themselves provoking the adolescent's problems nor seriously entangled in them. These parents may not wish to involve themselves in the treatment of their adolescent child; it is sufficient for them to know that the counselor is qualified to treat the adolescent.

In some other instances, usually with older adolescents, where the adolescent problem is truly an internal one, minimally intricated with parental neurosis, it is possible to conduct treatment with little communication with the parents. Sometimes the adolescent will request such confidentiality; it is then necessary to explain the procedure to the parents in order to maintain their cooperation. If it should ever become necessary to communicate with the parents, the adolescent should first be given an explanation for the necessity.

Parents who enter treatment because they are anxious about a child realize that it is centered on the adolescent but even though they are adults they may, in the beginning, fear the counselor, somewhat as adolescents do, because they anticipate criticism or blame for the errors they made in the upbringing of their child. Later, as the treatment progresses, they may come to understand that their initial fears contained transference elements from their own past. If parents continue, with the focus on their own problems, anxiety may arise again later, out of the fear of discovery of unacceptable impulses and the other usual anxieties which attend treatment.

A diagnostic formulation of family interaction and patterns informs the counselor of the primary parental and sibling forces in the adolescent's environment and how healthy or pathological these are. Where parents have supplied a fairly secure and warm relationship in the early years of life, and are puzzled and hurt by the adolescent's behavior, regarding him as strange, distant, secretive and unpredictable, their fears and angers can be viewed as reactions to current stress, and with some discussion and support, such parents will usually be cooperative in accepting treatment. As they come to understand their own reactions, they will see that they and the adolescent have come through previous developmental periods, and that for this particularly difficult phase solutions to troublesome behavior will also be reached with time and patience.

Where the parents were troubled during the child's early years of life, his fluctuating behavior in adolescence will probably be more frightening and overwhelming. Adolescents from such family interactions are frequently caught up in problems involving the total personality and strong internalization of conflict. The pull on the parents, and the reciprocal pull of parental conflicts on the adolescent, is indeed powerful. The parents may require more intensive treatment in which their rage, fear of dependency demands, their uneasiness and uncertainty for serving as identification objects, their fears of their own aggression and the aggression of the adolescent become expressed and accepted in an empathic relationship. But it is not essential to aim for major resolution of personality conflicts in the parents. Such a goal is not possible without a long period of time, and even if the time were available, such a goal would usually be strenuously resisted by the parents. They retain the right to determine what difficulties of their own they wish to see resolved, and it is wise to conform to the limits the parents set about their wish to change. The goal is to try to bolster ego strengths, to emphasize ways in which to act as a good mother or father, ways in which the adolescent can feel free to differentiate himself from his parents, and, most importantly, to urge consistent support of the adolescent's treatment.

Occasionally, the disorder of the parent is such that his behavior cannot be altered, or he is unwilling to make any efforts to change his handling of the adolescent, leaving all efforts toward change to the adolescent and his counselor. In these instances, the treatment plan for the adolescent may of necessity be a process of nurturing through to emancipation and natural separation.

In other cases where the parental character structure creates a situation in which pathological reactions of the adolescent are provoked, it may be necessary to arrange for placement of the adolescent away from the parents for any treatment to be effective. Unfortunately, in most communities there is a dearth of suitable residential resources for adolescents.

Different kind of parents and family problems require different treatment techniques although in each the central problem is that of the adolescent. In some instances, after a short diagnostic appraisal, the adolescent may be seen only at irregular intervals while treatment may focus on regular sessions with the mother. Gratified in her relationship with the counselor, the mother may be able to give more to her adolescent child, may be able to do a better job of mothering, and this increase in the parent's capacity to give may meet the adolescent's needs. Or, the main focus in treatment may be a father who needs help to be a more adequate male with the capacity to assume a more dominant role in his family.

The treatment must focus on what is uppermost in the current struggles of the parental interaction with the adolescent, and determine why failures occurred and what might be done to restore or structure effective functioning. The parents may be helped to repair superego defects, strengthening limits and controls in one area to deny the expression of primitive impulses, but relaxing them in others to permit experimentation and growth in areas of safety. The parents may be encouraged to use resources in the environment, school, peers, work, recreation, with careful consistent supervision. Everyday interaction should be examined in the interviews in specific ways to elicit the parents' own understanding which is then enlarged upon by the counselor in a systematic, patterned frame of reference so that the major themes are sensed and faced by the parents in the supportive relationship.

The counselor must like the adolescent and be sympathetic to his complaints about his parents. Almost all adolescents are critical of their parents but they feel threatened if others criticize them. It is not helpful to the treatment goals, for either parent or adolescent, for the counselor to join in the adolescent attacks upon the parents. Treatment aims at building, not undermining, the essential authority of the parental role in both the parent and the adolescent.

Involved in a sympathetic relationship with an adolescent, the counselor usually sees him once a week during which he can focus his entire attention upon the adolescent. The parent lives with the adolescent—and they can be very difficult—day by day, through all the harassment of life routines. The major responsibility for the welfare of the adolescent remains with the parent and the counselor keeps this fact in mind. He can be most helpful to the adolescent when he maintains an understanding attitude toward the parent and helps him to become a more effective parent.

# 12

# Identity Problems
# in Adolescence

THE HORMONAL CHANGES of puberty shake the stability of the preadolescent personality. As a result the adolescent finds both his mind and body are strange to him in many ways. New internal pressures, usually conflict-laden, are unfamiliar and he cannot immediately integrate the new feelings and experiences that are now part of himself. The ego feels estranged from itself, the adolescent develops a kind of objectivity toward his mind and his body as if they were not his own and his sense of identity becomes uncertain.

Adults have occasional fleeting experiences that give a glimpse into the identity confusions the adolescent feels. Now and then, walking down the street a person sees a reflection in a shop window and for a brief strange moment is not sure the figure he sees is himself. For that short instant his identity, his certain knowledge of himself, is shaken.

Adolescents live with this kind of uncertainty while they reevaluate all their previous experiences, question the meaning of their lives and the values of their environment. In order to achieve maturity the adolescent must reestablish a firm sense of identity.

The sense of self begins early in life. An infant begins to differentiate that which is himself from what is not himself with his first experiences, kinesthetic sensations arising out of body movements. An infant moves and has sensations which are immediate and real. He develops patterns of repeating these movements and re-senses the experiences. When an infant can voluntarily bring about movements he will do so, will repeat them because of the pleasure in the sensation itself and the sense of mastery that accompanies the accomplishment. By repetition, also, he learns what he can do and what he cannot do. Repetition gives a sense of reality to these experiences, makes them part of himself. The child finds that he has the capacity to will movements in his body and, further, that the will and the movements are his own. Some movements do not produce the desired effect and he gradually learns that a phenomenon that he cannot produce by his own will is non-self.

Many factors confuse these issues of self and non-self for the child. So much is necessarily done for the infant that he sometimes feels he can achieve a result without action or with minimal activity. He may merely need to salivate and he is fed. It is then difficult to separate what is I and what is not I. But by using the experience of putting various objects in his mouth, a cracker, a toy, or his own hand, and by experiencing different sensations, softness or hardness, cold or warmth, comfort when he is held, pain if he bites his own hand, he begins to learn the differences.

He is also confused at first about living objects; in the first stages the infant cannot separate himself from his mother. He cries. This produces gratifying feeding action on the part of the mother. The gratifying object, the mother, is felt as part of himself. Normal identification has its source in this experience.

Once the early experiences of the self have differentiated the I from the non-I, in the first few months of life, identity begins to become established. Then interpersonal relationships complicate the process of creating a self-identity. Some parents set

conditions too early and do not allow an infant the time or freedom to be himself. The infant puts his hand in his mouth, enjoys
the sucking and the power and success of having willed his hand
to go into his mouth. But if the parents set conditions on what
may be experienced and enjoyed, if they do not consider it
acceptable to suck, the parents will remove the infant's hand
from his mouth. The infant then has to deal with a conflict. He
wants to suck his hands but he cannot do so with the parents
present. Eventually his wish to suck is repressed and labeled
"not myself." Observed from outside, by others, this impulse
is still present, but it is not contained within his sense of identity.

These early conflicts with the immediate environment are the
basis of pathology or of healthy emotional development; pathology if the basic urge must be repressed, made non-self; health
if the basic urge can be directed in some way to satisfy the
environment and still continue as part of the self.

As the child comes to feel his dependence on people outside
of himself, he begins to learn from them what he should be.
People label the child or his actions in one way or another and
the attitude conveyed by the labeling is added or not added to
the sense of self. "I am good." "I am bad."

Parents may help or hinder the process of making primary
experiences part of the child's self. Parents may, for example,
exclaim over an infant girl's prettiness; the baby experiences her
own body, plus the glowing positive sensation of being loved
and admired. This adulation becomes an important part of her
experience and she grows up with the feeling that she is pretty.
The pretty baby may become a homely adolescent and she
then has to match her inner feeling of prettiness against the
reality of not being good-looking. An emotionally healthy adolescent can recognize the reality that she is no longer pretty
while retaining the inner feeling of prettiness. On the other
hand, there are very pretty adolescent girls who do not accept
the reality of their good looks, who have no feeling of attractiveness. Out of a different set of childhood experiences, they

developed a sense of self which included ugliness of body or personality.

In the same way an individual who thinks of himself as a good person, although he has had experiences which are good and some that are not good, has included within himself only the good as his own identity. He does not accept what is bad as part of the totality of himself.

The sense of self and of identity is preconscious but it can at any moment be brought into consciousness. It is difficult to state what an individual is aware of as belonging to his own identity, because the sense of self supersedes all the details which it embodies. It is the outcome of putting together the total life experiences with the addition, "This is mine, this belongs to me, this is I." The sense of identity is an integrated feeling of a special quality, the uniqueness of one's own self. In order to describe this feeling it must be broken down into its significant aspects.

One can be certain of a sense of self and yet have difficulty pinpointing its components. It includes the body but a person can lose a limb or other parts of the body and still retain an undamaged sense of self.

Occasionally everyone has the experience of doing something strange and asking himself why he did what he did. The very question carries the implication that the bizarre act is not acknowledged as part of the sense of self. If the act is studied or analyzed it will be found that the motivation was unconscious. The sense of self is a conviction which ordinarily is not questioned. When it is solid and well integrated it continues under many toxic or pathological conditions. Even in serious illness, with delirium, the self can be sensed as experiencing the delirious state. It is possible in emotional illness, psychosis or neurosis, still to feel the conviction of the self experiencing the pathological phenomena. In amnesia there is a loss of knowledge of the details that apply to the identity but the amnesiac has a sense of himself without being able to name that self.

During loss of consciousness, there is no sense of self. And there are some psychotic states in which there is a loss of identity. In severe depressions the self may feel strange to the individual.

Some experiences may be repressed and the individual then has a constant sense of something missing. In the hysterias, for example, the experiences of which the body is capable have been repressed out of fear and a full sense of the wholeness of the self is lacking.

Additional experiences are incorporated into the sense of self as they occur. Many people, for example, have difficulty recognizing their own voices the first time they hear them mechanically recorded. Subsequently, however, the recorded voice is accepted as part of themselves, integrated into the self.

All the experiences which people undergo in life, from the moment of becoming an experiencing organism, are self experiences which gradually become integrated into that which they describe as themselves. Each individual has a unique sense of self which evolved out of his own experience. A person is certain of his sense of existence and of his life as being his own.

The sense of self involves three aspects of identity. The first is the social objective identity which is the final outcome of the personality development as seen by or manifested to others. The second is personal objective identity, the way an individual perceives himself, based on his observations of himself.

The third is the subjective identity which is the individual's feeling of the continuity of himself, superseding what others see or even what he himself perceives about himself. This subjective identity is a feeling of the self composed of familiarity with body and psychological experiences. It may be at variance with both kinds of objective identity, as with the homely girl who continues to feel pretty. It may, in some instances, coincide with the personal objective identity which is the individual's own observations about himself. But it rarely coincides with the social objective identity. People seldom see themselves as others see them and the differences are greater in adolescence.

The variance between subjective and objective aspects of identity is readily seen in relation to occupational choice. A man's objective identity may include the fact that he is a lawyer or a carpenter, but his subjective sense of self would remain the same if he were to change to another kind of employment. In some few vocations, such as the creative arts, religious callings, or other service professions and some types of professional athletics, an individual has the opportunity to feel very intensely that his objective identity is also his sensed self. This coincidence of subjective and objective identity is fortunate when it occurs in a socially acceptable manner.

The sense of self is built out of motoric functions, from the development of feelings and experiences through the five senses; objective identity is developed through external definitions such as sex, appearance and behavior which contribute to the self-image. By the time of latency, subjective and objective identity are grossly settled. A child is by this time a little lady or a tomboy, a sissy, or a roughneck. He has a crystallized image of himself coinciding with most of his childhood character.

With the onset of adolescence, attitudes and values are undermined and the stability of identity is lost. Most adolescents modify their objective sense of self but maintain the subjective identity. The adolescent goes through a period of observing his body and its sensations as if these were not part of himself. Only when he becomes certain that the new body and emotional feelings are himself and can accept this newness as himself, does he achieve a real sense of identity. While most adolescents undergo some identity destabilization they remain relatively constant in their sense of identity and they usually arrive at a state of integration by the end of the second decade. When the adolescent does not find a solution he goes through a more or less acute episode of disturbance in the integration of the personality in which the chief theme is the loss of a solid and secure sense of identity.

## IDENTITY DIFFUSION

The state of disorganization in relation to the self which may occur in adolescence has been named identity diffusion by Eric Erikson. This condition is a pathology of adolescence because the primary task of this developmental phase is the integration of personality. Every pathology contains disintegration but none of the specific pathologies as they are ordinarily classified adequately describes this adolescent disorder. The condition most closely resembles an acute schizophrenic reaction of a non-specific nature but adolescents with identity diffusion are not psychotic if they maintain a hold on reality. When the state is acute and transitional it is called identity crisis, but the term identity diffusion places more emphasis on the important dynamics of the adolescent's own sensing that he does not know himself during this phase.

An adolescent in a state of identity diffusion has reactivated many of the tensions of early developmental conflict. The old ego ideal is challenged so that the purposes and goals of life are not merely questioned, but may even be abandoned. Within relatively short periods of time such an adolescent may flit from acting out on impulse to enforcing rigid self-control. He is momentarily flooded with impulse and then defends against it. His superego is ineffective and inconsistent, as the adolescent alternates between giving into his impulses and strictly curbing them. Impulses reveal themselves and may be acted upon suddenly. The ego is caught between this vacillating superego and impulsivity. The defensive structure is inconsistent. The inconsistency itself characterizes the diffused identity state.

Some adolescents cannot adequately describe the feeling of diffusion but others are able to say directly that they do not know who they are. However, a sense of identity remains, even though it is unconscious, and serves to prevent disintegration.

The adolescents most likely to develop identity diffusion are those who have had conflict-laden childhoods where the earlier developmental phases were traumatic. If the diffusion of identity is not resolved during adolescence the result may be a prolonged adolescent personality, an adult who leads his life in an adolescent manner. The "adolescent" adult will be somewhat more systematic, settling into the loose patterns with somewhat less tendency to extremes than the actual adolescent because a degree of quiescence occurs with the passage of years.

Almost all adolescents feel that society's expectations are not naturally and necessarily a part of themselves. Cultural standards originate from outside the individual. Often behavior which conforms to society's expectations feels strange to an adolescent and though he may attempt to do what is required of him he has a continuous lack of conviction. The adolescent with identity diffusion carries this sense of not being convinced to an extreme; everything feels "phoney."

Identity diffusion may be more common in boys than in girls, perhaps because girls have direction spelled out for them more clearly than do boys. Biological fulfillment is more gratifying than cultural fulfillment, and child bearing and rearing are primary concerns of females. In this sense girls have a more definite aim to their lives and are not so apt to get lost amid drifting boundaries. Girls integrate into young womanhood earlier than boys into manhood.

The continual questioning, the re-evaluative process, and the degree to which it is carried on, are important components of the identity diffusion. Looking for identity involves searching for values. In any therapeutic relationship the adolescent looks for and takes on the values of his counselor as his new ego ideal, but with the adolescent in a state of identity diffusion who is scrutinizing and questioning all of his own values, the identification with the counselor is a more urgent process.

Adolescent identity diffusion does not usually develop into psychosis. For psychosis to occur there must be a serious defect in the ego. The identity diffused adolescent most frequently has a basic internal integrity which the counselor may observe even if the adolescent himself cannot. In identity diffusion, while the ego has difficulty coping with the supergeo and the impulses, there is often a saving defensive maneuver of being able to stand off to observe the process. This self-observation is a definite asset for surviving the critical period. Adolescents with this technique of self-observation are often talkative which in itself is an aid to treatment.

The factors which serve to hold together an adolescent with identity diffusion, and keep him from breakdown are: 1) his hold on reality; 2) his persistent sense of self, however confused temporarily; 3) clues or guidelines picked up from the external environment which serve to dictate his behavior or activities; 4) his understanding that he is undergoing a temporary adolescent process; 5) the hope for integration.

## Differentiation from Psychosis

It is clinically possible to find similar defensive structure and malfunctioning in the psychotic adolescent and in one with identity diffusion. The counselor's impression of the total personality is an important factor in the differentiation. An intimate contact over a number of interviews conveys a feeling of the nature of total personality and this impression is often more accurate than a listing of ego mechanisms or defenses. The counselor will sense that the adolescent in identity diffusion is not bizarre, withdrawn, incomprehensible or isolated. All ego defenses are loosened in identity diffusion and whatever may be expected in normal adolescence occurs more often and more abruptly in the adolescent with identity diffusion. The general impression is that this adolescent differs from other adolescents only quantitatively; he is, in effect, "more" adolescent. Still, a fundamental integration in the personality is communicated which is missing in the psychotic.

The adolescent in identity diffusion has an active need for relationships, wants to be involved, and continues to search for relationship. The psychotic may also want a relationship but he cannot persist in his search. The counselor senses a distance from himself in the immediate interview situation with the psychotic. The adolescent with identity diffusion is reacting within the same emotional orbit as the counselor.

In the psychotic there is a difference in the quality of communication which the counselor recognizes although not necessarily by a conscious process. Differences are subtle and the counselor's awareness may be on a feeling level, rather than conscious or intellectual. But even untrained people who pay close attention can sense the strangeness in the communications of the psychotic.

Rigidity, stereotypy and persistence of ideas and affects mark the psychotic; whatever peculiarities exist in the identity-diffused adolescent shift and are not continuous.

The adolescent in identity diffusion may have abnormal perceptions transiently but psychotics persist in hallucinations and in preoccupation with their inner perceptions. Any individual may, at a given time, be preoccupied with his own inner life, and a neurotic adolescent in identity diffusion may even have an occasional hallucinatory experience. But a nonpsychotic adolescent finds hallucination ego alien and when he has such an experience he considers it so strange and frightening that he may panic. At first, the psychotic adolescent may also be frightened by his hallucinatory experiences but as they continue he will begin to use the experience itself as an adaptive mechanism. The psychotic personality integrates on a psychotic level while for the identity-diffused adolescent such experiences continue to remain alien and strange. Instead of integrating such phenomena the neurotic will try to defend against them.

The major diagnostic clue in differentiating the psychotic from the adolescent with identity diffusion is the integration of the core personality. Differentiation is important because factors in treatment differ between the adolescent in identity diffusion and the adolescent who is psychotic.

## Treatment

The basic goal in the treatment of identity diffusion is the reintegration of the personality. The counselor uses those techniques which help toward his goal: he gives direction and indicates there is organization within the adolescent's personality; he lets the adolescent know that he is searching for a goal which can be attained; he permits himself to be used by the adolescent as a guide toward that goal.

The adolescent suffering from identity diffusion cannot endure his state of chronic doubt. He wants answers immediately; he feels he cannot exist without final answers. But the counselor cannot help him by providing answers. The counselor offers hope for later fulfillment as a method of handling the adolescent's many questions. The adolescent is told that in time he will find the answers for himself. The constant questions are for the purpose of defense and the counselor never attacks a defense. In reality, integration comes through the unconscious fulfillment in the therapeutic relationship, not through answers to questions. Life becomes meaningful ordinarily in infancy through relationships and repetitively throughout life, with specially urgent need for relationship in adolescence.

The adolescent in identity diffusion offers many rationalizations, argues desperately and may be preoccupied with philosophic theorizing. The counselor keeps focused on the goal and avoids being led into arguments or discussions. An attempt to answer the numerous questions raised by the adolescent only increases the anxiety since there are no satisfying answers. The primary objective is that the adolescent's personality must find direction and direction is found in integration. Later in life, from the solid footing of his personality integration, an adult may question the values of society, his own aims and goals, or may want to make changes and accommodations in the world around him. But adults have learned to accept that in spite of less than complete fulfillment they must make life as gratifying as possible. Adolescents find this difficult to accept.

The counselor uses himself as the therapeutic tool for the purpose of reintegrating the adolescent. The treatment of an adolescent in identity diffusion is not a simple task, the course is rough and much time is involved. It takes time for the relationship to become meaningful. This type of adolescent is cynical and distrustful; he may see all adults as fools, conformists to a false world which he finds without meaning. He engages in a good deal of testing in treatment. But basically he has the need for relationship; treatment is built on this need and succeeds if the relationship is gratifying.

Adolescents who lived with conflict-laden early relationships with their parents do not readily feel trust. The child who has been loved has a basic confidence that human beings can provide fulfillment. Questioning values is a common phenomenon of all adolescents, but the gratified child responds to love and affection even while he is questioning all the standards by which he lives. The adolescent whose infancy was disturbed has a more difficult time in treatment because has no confidence that another human being can understand or fulfill his needs. The effectiveness of treatment always depends on earlier relationships. An adolescent whose earlier life experiences were good can benefit more readily from treatment. When his relationships have not been good, he is fearful that if he "submits" he will lose his integrity and his freedom to be himself.

The counselor creates a positive atmosphere with the adolescent, accepts him, works with the hope of fulfillment and the confidence that there can be direction to the personality. Because the adolescent in identity diffusion lacks direction, is distressed, confused and anxious, the counselor must be unanxious, confident and constant, gradually building a sense of trust within the relationship. In the beginning of treatment it is difficult to determine what issue or issues have thrown the adolescent into the state of diffusion. There may be no one simple psychodynamic issue and generalizations are not possible except that adolescence itself, and the press of the problems of heterosexuality are commonly the precipitating factors. In each specific instance the counselor searches for the particular struggle which precipitated the diffusion.

At the beginning of treatment the counselor indicates to the diffused adolescent that he will try to understand him. This is done not for insight alone but for intellectual control over the diffused state. It also holds out hope for solution. The counselor listens attentively and looks for a point at which he can intervene to give some direction. He induces the adolescent to talk about specific problems and searches for a time in the adolescent's life when there was focus and integration, using that fixed point for help in the present. He affirms confidence that resolution and solution will come and calms the adolescent by urging patience in order to give treatment a chance. Listening carefully, showing interest, helping in specific ways and making specific suggestions about the management of life all appeal to the adolescent's need for stability and relationships. In these ways the counselor makes himself important to the adolescent. The prototype is the good parent-child relationship. Intervention, when necessary, in specific difficult areas at home or at school proves the counselor's interest in his welfare.

At the start of treatment these adolescents may have negative affects which the counselor recognizes as part of the diffusion. The counselor does not play a superego role. He does not condone unacceptable activities but he is sympathetic to the idea that it is universal to have unacceptable impulses. Superego issues are de-emphasized particularly in relation to social and school behavior. It is more therapeutic to err on the side of being benign than being disciplinary in order to win over the disturbed and confused adolescent.

After the initial phases of treatment with the identity-diffused adolescent and when some integration has occurred, the next phase in treatment depends on the specific pathology or state of personality disorder which underlies the diffusion. Treatment then proceds in the usual manner.

# 13

# Learning Problems Related to Character Formation

MANY SERIOUS PROBLEMS exist in the public schools, racial, social, and economic as well as educational. Penetrating questions are being raised about the traditional curriculum, about inequities in opportunity, about parental participation in educational decision-making, about qualifications of teachers and administrators. The customary measurements of intellectual potential are being challenged; the track system has defenders and detractors. Library shelves are filled with volumes on why children do not learn to read and the disciples of various methods for teaching the basic skills hotly dispute each other. The physically and mentally handicapped require improved facilities which are not always available. The mentally retarded need special educational techniques. More refined methods of diagnosis can identify organic disorders and minimal brain damage early, and skilled teaching methods reduce the educational disabilities of these handicaps. If development within the first few years of life is significantly disturbed the capacity for learning may be irreparably damaged. The learning disabilities of many underprivileged children stem from this deprivation. These varied mass problems call for the co-operation of government, local communities, educators and the expertise of specialists in many fields.

All young adolescents are affected by the educational system. They are aware of the criticisms directed at the schools and suffer from the deficiencies. Inadequacies in preparation make it difficult or impossible for a student to function in high school. Curricula irrelevant to present-day needs will not stimulate student interest. When any high school student needs help for emotional problems, his school functioning and the realities of his particular school situation should be understood by the counselor as an important part of the fabric of the adolescent's life.

But even under optimum school conditions a combination of factors related to the adolescent process itself tends to create learning problems in high school, especially in large public school systems. These are: the onset of puberty; change from grade school, and close association with a relatively constant group of classmates and one or a few teachers to the more impersonal high school environment; the curriculum or subject orientation of high school as contrasted with the teacher-student relationship of the grade school; exposure to a large group of older, more sexually advanced schoolmates; the change from the smaller school in the immediate neighborhood to the larger, and usually more distantly located high school.

In some communities where the junior high school is used as a transition it has been observed that postponement, not easing, of these issues results. The same situations arise at the time of the transfer from the jnuior to the senior high school.

School personnel usually are prepared to cope with the ordinary adolescent reactions, the freshman bewilderment or the sophomore slump. But some kinds of school problems cannot be handled by educational methods because they are interrelated with the characteristic functioning of the whole personality. The difficulties in learning are the observable symptom; the problem lies within the adolescent's personality. Adolescent learning problems arising out of intrapsychic conflict should be differentiated from other educational problems because treatment must be directed to the personality structure of the adolescent. Changes in the educational process will have only minimal effect when the basis for the difficulty lies within the individual's own personality.

Many adolescents are referred for specialized counseling because of learning problems, chiefly underachievement, which is readily identifiable and of much concern to parents and educators. The adolescent who invests most of his energy in school achievement, even to the exclusion of other areas of development, is not generally considered to have problems; neither his school nor his home are as quick to consider the personality factors in this concentration. But the student with good intellectual capacity who is a behavior problem in the classroom or who does mediocre or failing work is a source of great concern; usually the failure to learn is considered the major problem rather than recognized as one symptom of personality disturbance.

Adolescents whose problems in learning are rooted in psychological conflict can be divided into the following groups:

Some adolescents displace home problems onto the school with the conscious awareness that poor performance or school failure is the most severe form of attack or retaliation against their parents within the adolescents' power.

There are adolescents who displace the home struggles onto the school without conscious awareness, usually in such a manner that specific aspects of class and classroom take on a special meaning. For example, an individual teacher may be unconsciously equated with a parent.

The overwhelming importance of sexuality, or of relationships to overcome feelings of loneliness, may serve to relegate education to an insignificant or minor position in the life of the adolescent with libidinal drives assuming primary interest. This may be true even of older adolescents, many of whom attend college for reasons not related to actual learning, such as for social status, or for the purpose of finding a mate.

There are adolescents who have little capacity for sublimation. Learning is an ego function whose ultimate purpose is mastery of the environment for survival. But for many people it is also extremely valuable as a mode of sublimation of primitive psychological urges, as well as for draining off libido, anxieties or tensions from conflict. Adolescents whose lives have forced them to seek gratification of the basic psychobiological impulses or have offered no opportunity for channeling these impulses continue to be preoccupied with these impulses to such a degree that learning is a drudgery which has no sublimatory function.

There are adolescents whose learning difficulties relate to specific subject matter which has unconscious meaning related to the individual personality structure. They may have so much anxiety around a special area that they cannot learn that particular subject. For example, the son of an English teacher could not learn grammar for the unconscious purpose of defeating himself as a resolution of the oedipal conflict. Both boys and girls may have difficulty with biology because of the sexual implications of that field of study. Many girls unconsciously equate the ability to think abstractly with masculinity. For this reason mathematics may present special problems for them. Academically achieving girls may perhaps be those who have identified with their fathers.

In some instances, the adolescent rebellion takes the form of refusing to perform whatever is expected of them, chiefly because it is required. Special rebels, usually intellectually capable, scorn grades and refuse to work for them. They may learn the subject matter more than adequately yet refuse to comply with the specific requirements which affect the final grading; they may carry this to the point of choosing to fail rather than yield.

Adolescents with compulsive character formations may become absorbed in procedural methods to the exclusion of the learning itself. Some adolescents unconsciously rebel against the superego edict to learn by time-consuming involvement in details and procedural rituals.

Some adolescents have unconsciously determined anxiety specifically related to education which prevents them from attending school. Separation from parents, some meaning attached to the teacher, the school environment, the subject matter or the process of education itself may have created a true clinical phobia.

There are adolescents who see no value in the educational process. The sense of value in education need not necessarily relate to the cultural standards of the adolescent's home or immediate environment. Adolescents from culturally deprived homes may have a strong sense of the worth of education while others with educated parents may not find value for themselves in education. The worth or lack of worth of educuation is a reflection of the adolescent's own feeling about its meaning to himself.

Where the ego function of cognition is defective and when the integration of perceived facts is not possible, students cannot learn because they do not have the ego capacity to profit from educational material in an ordinarily meaningful way.

Other students display marked discrepancy between aspiration or drive and ability. They may either grossly underrate or overrate their capacity for achievement in a manner that interferes with actual learning progress.

Characterologically the problem is one in which the concept of the learning self is a distorted one.

No adolescent problem originates with the onset of puberty; problems have their roots in the unresolved conflicts of earlier developmental phases. In order to be effective, treatment must be aimed at the underlying dynamic structure rather than exclusively at the present learning difficulty. The type of learning problem reveals the residuals of earlier developmental issues and learning problems can be categorized by the developmental levels from which they originate.

## LEARNING PROBLEMS ARISING OUT OF EARLY EGO PHASE OF DEVELOPMENT

### Defects in the Autonomous Ego Process

Some difficulties in learning relate to failures in development of the ego during the early phase of life during which the structuring of the ego begins. The whole personality may not be fixated at this point; only one or another aspect may be fixated or remnants of the early developmental problems may remain in the personality.

Human beings are born with the capacity to perceive the world and make it meaningful unless mental retardation or organic defects of the cortex create difficulties in perception, memory and association.

Autonomous functions may be interfered with very early; the ways in which mothers handle infants may enhance or inhibit autonomous ego functioning and have subsequent effects on learning. If early sensations and perceptions are painful and unpalatable the development even of perception as an autonomous function may be defective.

### Schizoid Learners—Thinking Disorders

Learning problems arise out of the whole personality in schizophrenia but schizoid traits may affect learning in a number of ways. Thinking disorders interfere with the ability to use secondary processes such as normal logic. Schizoid disorders allow the intrusion of fantasy and unconscious thought into the mind, sometimes subliminally, often consciously. Affective disorders may cause withdrawal or apathy with loss of emotional involvement in learning. Schizoid reactions sometimes occur due to the pressures of adolescence; the learning problem then is a part of the total emotional disorder.

## Inability to Sublimate into Learning

Early ego functions cannot be learned. The individual is born with certain capacities which are enhanced or deterred by the environment. Sublimation is an ego function which is related to the earliest phase of ego development although it does not manifest itself early in life. Sublimation becomes most evident in latency when the impulses tend to be controlled and there is a further flowering in adolescence. Although sublimation manifests itself consciously the individual is not aware of all that goes into its making. The capacity for sublimation may be an innate quality and its lack may be an ego defect.

Libidinal interests cannot be forced to move in any desired direction although they may be encouraged. For example, if sexual curiosity is inhibited by the parents in a home where there are books, it is possible that the interest may be rechanneled from sexual curiosity into reading. The channelization is an autonomous function of the ego and some people do not have this capacity to rechannel. Some children whose sexual curiosity is inhibited cannot use reading or learning as a source of gratification.

In some instances sublimation can be fostered by suppression of impulse. For example, when the hostile impulses are prohibted by parental demand, a child may sublimate by becoming interested in athletic activities or by reading science fiction or adventure stories or by the use of intellectualization. The acting-out child has not been able to sublimate aggressive impulses adequately.

Sublimation is not merely substitution and substitution does not necessarily lead to sublimation. In child rearing, however, substitution is the beginning process which may foster sublimation if the potential is present. A parent may give a child a drum to beat as a substitute for destructive hitting with a stick, and creating the rhythmic sound may become a sublimation. Sublimation is usually constructive and acceptable to the culture although it is possible that an individual may be involved in a sublimation that others would consider inferior or of little value. Learning is a sublimation for many people. Others do not have the capacity to sublimate in learning.

## LEARNING PROBLEMS ARISING OUT OF ORAL PHASE OF DEVELOPMENT

### Passive and Dependent Learners

Dependent learners learn for the sake of possessing the teacher in the way that an infant wishes to possess his mother. The type of interaction with the teacher depends on the individual dynamics. In the passive learner it may be simple dependency or there may be guilt over dependency which constricts learning. These submissive takers may have a feeling of obligation to the teacher and do what is required of them as a means of winning the teacher's love.

Passive learners may learn through supportive identification, a process of osmosis. They are dependent upon identification with the teacher and are not free to feel, think or act independently or creatively.

Some osmotic learners have high intelligence, but they are unwilling to work. They have acquired methods of getting along with minimal effort; they take in what is given out by the teacher, and may actually acquire information, but what they learn does not have the same meaning as learning which is integrated as part of one's self. These students do not appear rivalrous, their hostility is not apparent and they seem to have flexible superegos. They are in school to please an external agent rather than because of an interest in education. They are not likely to question whatever is handed out to them. Their dependence on those who nurture them limits their capacity to integrate learning.

Another type of passive learner is the student who remains on the periphery. He appears to adapt but the adaptation is only superficial. He keeps putting out feelers for cues as to the best way to get along. He does not usually seem anxious, possibly because he is never deeply engaged.

With all of these orally dependent learners, the passive dependent, the osmotic learner and the peripheral learner, there is no true investment in or integration of the subject matter. They continue to relate on the subject level the way infants do. They feel they have no right to question but must be passive and submissive. They have unfulfilled dependency needs and their unconscious hostility over not getting gratification makes it difficult for them to derive much value out of education.

Dependent learners also share a superego problem. The superego as it relates to learning is external rather internalized. They comply or annex but do not integrate. Although they demand the affection of the teacher they readily abandon one teacher for another as a young infant relates to any mothering figure. These students may adjust to reality demands; they may even succeed in some areas, but learning is not basically adaptive, not truly part of themselves. Learning is an external idea to which they are subjected. There may be varying degrees of hostility, rebellion or compliance.

For treatment purposes it is necessary to determine how an individual adolescent functions, what is internalized and what is not, how much is internalized, and how the individual learning patterns are modified in terms of current realities. It is important to know whether the adolescent places intrinsic value on learning, how dependent he is on relationships in order to be able to learn, and how much the compliance to learn is merely appeasement of the superego.

Many superego issues create guilt; some are internalized and some are not. A dependent learner who must also arrange his desk neatly before he can begin to study may have internalized superego issues of cleanliness and neatness while learning remains an external superego issue, not internalized.

Adolescence offers a second chance at integration of issues dealing with relationships, reshifting from earlier forms of relationships and behavior and coming to terms with reality. It is a time of loosening of old pressures and of the integrations used in the past. The outcome depends in large part on how adaptive an individual was in earlier phases. If internalization and integration seemed too dangerous earlier, they will appear too dangerous in adolescence and the adolescent will need help before he is able to risk making changes in his customary patterns. A child who had adapted well earlier, in adolescence can re-evaluate for himself and give up earlier adaptations which are not functioning successfully.

## Oral Aggressive Learners

The oral aggressive learner differs from the passive dependent learner in that he is more interested in actively seeking the love of the teacher. For both, wholehearted approval assumes major importance and determines the motivation for school performance. But the aggressive learner makes an effort, throws his aggressions into the learning process. He may sometimes be a hard-working student and can sometimes appear to be a successful learner. The aggression is manifested in the classroom by attention getting devices, constant hand-raising, arguing, sometimes battling the teacher. Anything serves that the aggressive student thinks will gain the approbation of the teacher.

With oral aggressive students the learning itself may suffer because they do not have adequate judgment about what is important. Their technique is to gobble everything that is put before them indiscriminately. When these students argue in class, there is a hostile quality to their affect which makes the perceptive teacher aware that they are really fighting the teacher and the other students, not debating ideas. They can become classroom nuisances, taking up the time of the whole class in argument and fruitless discussion. Yet out of this aggressive learning pattern there can develop an accumulation of learning which may eventually be integrated.

Mature students are interested in the material and not merely in the reactions of the teacher; they can learn from a person who shows no personal interest or from one who presents material in a dull or even a boring manner. To be overly interested in securing the love of the teacher, or getting grades as symbols of love or lovableness, is a manifestation of unresolved oral dependency needs. Aggressive attempts to get the love of the teacher or aggressive competition with classmates or the teacher are expressions of hostile competitive attitudes displaced from siblings and parents.

The excessive need for love is primarily due to an inadequate self-esteem and a low estimate of personal worth. Self-esteem accrues to a loved infant on a nonverbal, purely affectional basis. This built-in feeling of lovableness and worth can never be added later in life in the same way or with the same unconditional quality. Oral aggressive learners want approval because they need it as the measure of their own value. The reasons why a child is left with the feeling that he still needs love which was not given him earlier are numerous and range all the way from identification with an inadequate parent to actual physical abuse. Frequently this excessive need for affection is the outcome of a difficult sibling situation with persistent hostile rivalries and what appeared to the child to be an unfair distribution of parental love.

There are oral aggressive students who have given up striving and instead seem to look for disapproval and failure. These are depressed personalities. They have given up trying to obtain the love they want, therefore they have given up learning; they have no motivation for learning. Since they feel they have always failed to get love, they see no reason for continuing the attempt to get it. These students too may be disruptive in class and may fight the teacher in denial of their need for love and approval or as an expression of hostility over frustrations.

Some aggressive learners who are latently depressed are intensely searching for a relationship in order to avoid depression. They desperately want approval; if the approval is not forthcoming they then suffer depression. If the ego is strong enough to withstand pain, they may not become profoundly depressed and may still be able to function. They may become resigned to the frustrations of their life situation and to their deprivations.

As adults they may learn to accept such a life situation. They become characterologically depressed but are not *in* a depression. The depressive affects are present but the structure of the personality is maintained. They do not give up their values but the motivation for striving for love from another no longer is present. This depressive orientation is common. There is, after all, no complete gratification for anyone and almost every adolescent develops some questioning about his worth.

The adolescent who has given up completely is seriously disturbed emotionally. Ordinarily adolescents are hopeful and even those who are depressed still retain hopes for eventual gratification. In treatment this hope can be mobilized to build a measure of self-esteem, though the structure may remain fragile, in need of constant bolstering, and may never be as solid as the self-esteem of the child who felt adequately loved in infancy.

In the depths of a clinical depression the student with an oral character formation cannot learn; he feels that he has failed to gain love and since this was his motivation for learning he no longer can learn. Some adolescents who manifest delinquent behavior and are poor school achievers are, in actuality, oral depressed personalities.

### LEARNING PROBLEMS ARISING OUT OF ANAL PHASE OF DEVELOPMENT

The first systematic education of a child begins with training for bowel control, usually sometime between the ages of one and a half and three. Rarely in life are any demands imposed as consistently by time, place, and method as are the issues of anal training. Around toilet training for the first time the child consciously faces the struggle over meeting the expectation of others, learns self-mastery and contends with principles. The process of learning bowel control requires a great deal of the child. He makes the decision as to whether or not he will fulfill the expectations placed on him. If negative feelings outweigh the positive feelings of goodness and love, and if the child feels negatively about producing for his parents, then he may subsequently resist other requirements imposed by parents or parent surrogates.

In modern Western culture discipline first relates to anality; the anal issues becomes pattern-setting and determines many other kinds of self-control. Each developmental phase may create conflict in any personality but the more integrated the developmental residuals are, the more favorable the foundation for motivation for learning. Learning techniques which arise out of the anal phase may be good techniques if they are tempered with flexibility and good ego perception. However, anal phase conflict can make for certain learning problems in adolescence. Superego problems in relation to authority, and learning with the emphasis on methods rather than purposes may be the outcome of such conflict.

Some adolescents are consciously aware of their rebellion

against parental pressures to achieve in school. In defiance of parental authority and superego edicts the adolescent yields to his own inclinations. Defiance contains elements of hostility and vengeance; motivation for rebellious defiance varies. It may arise from oral sadism when it takes such forms as sarcasm, but stubbornness is rooted in anal defiance. Stubborn defiant students refuse to study; they often will not hand in assigned work and they refuse to learn.

Unconscious defiance takes various forms. Some adolescents forget or omit assignments, instructions, and sections of examinations. Others need to postpone studying until superego edicts are fulfilled in rituals, such as straightening the desk, sharpening pencils, or organizing work materials. Still others show regressive longings when faced with the demand to study; they get hungry or thirsty and must interrupt their work frequently to raid the refrigerator. Some students wander off into fantasy when they start to read the textbook.

Resistance to superego pressures to learn results in several kinds of learning dysfunction. Some students are procrastinators, fighting with inner resistance until the last possible moment; then, under the threat of a deadline, they may produce what is required. They may be conscious of the defiance but often are not conscious of their motives for resistance to superego injunction.

Perfectionism is an obsessive compulsive technique used without direct defiance of superego pressure. Certain learning techniques used excessively become ends in themselves. Students of this kind may be able to learn thoroughly and well but their methods interfere with the progress of learning and the required expectations. They may do such extensive preparation for a paper that it is not completed in time or they may miss the focus of the assignment through over-use of detail. The internal need for orderliness and careful procedure makes it impossible to keep up with the normal learning expectation. Consciously these rituals are in the service of learning, but emphasis on the details interferes with accomplishment; the superego overrules the ego.

Passive aggressive learners can also be defiant through compliance itself. This kind of student may be inordinately slow in doing his required work or habitually late in completing assignments. When urged or appealed to he appears aggrieved and has the ready answer, "But I *am* doing it." These students are quiet in class but uninterested and frequently distracted. They do not openly disobey; they may behave only too well, but they learn very little.

Conscious anxiety over anal failure is another source of learning problems. These students become overwhelmed with anxieties that they will not be able to fulfill the superego demands. Such excessive anxiety may exist around a particular subject of study, a single topic, or an individual teacher. Sometimes a teacher, reacting to the sensed stubbornness, will insist that the student produce. The teacher presses and the student cannot give. Then the anxiety can become overwhelming, may approach a panic state and can actually result in failure. The causation relates to childhood threats of punishment and the fear of what may hapepn if there is no bowel production at the stipulated time and place.

The treatment of learning problems which develop out of residual anal conflict is difficult by reason of the resistance to superego and because of the ego techniques used for defiance. If the superego has become internalized it is harder to affect the adolescent with poor learning techniques. The counselor may be able to be patient when he realizes that the stubbornness and the strength invested in these techniques arise out of an infantile survival need for mastery in order to be autonomous.

## LEARNING PROBLEMS ARISING OUT OF OEDIPAL PHASE OF DEVELOPMENT

As an individual progresses in his development the residuals of earlier stages remain and continue to have influence, though modified by later stages.

In the oedipal phase the child sees himself as a complete person; he thinks about himself in comparison with the adults around him, as a little woman or a little man. Under benign circumstances he looks on himself as a potential adult with an urge toward success. The child's own self-estimation leads him to want to do more than he actually can do at this time. The boy child wants to be a man, like his father, the girl a woman, like her mother. This desire to take over the parent's role includes sexuality.

At this period in development there is a great interest in almost everything, great curiosity which extends from body function to cosmic concepts. The oedipal phase involves more than sexual impulses; it includes the wish for mastery of all the adult functions the child observes. Physical contacts with the parents become enmeshed in this heightened curiosity and the child develops a different kind of awareness of his own body because in his physical development he is now able to experience genital sensation.

Sexuality is only one issue about which the child is curious. But because of adults' feelings about sexuality this one aspect of the wish to know may be inhibited or exaggerated. Blocks to curiosity result in learning problems. If the curiosity becomes conflictual the child begins to wonder if it is right to want to know.

A child whose questions about the genitalia of the opposite sex are treated as if they were "bad" may connect the parental disapproval with the questioning as well as the specific subject. To question, then, is to be bad and the child inhibits his curiosity, not only about sexual matters.

What a child selects as the specific conflict area and how he equates this to some area of learning depend on the special circumstances of his development and life history. One boy of good intelligence had not been able to learn to read by the age of nine. In treatment it was revealed that he entered first grade shortly after the birth of a sister. By coincidence the first reading lesson in school showed a picture of a cuddly little infant girl with the letters B-A-B-Y under it. His sibling rivalry and conflict about baby girls blocked this boy so that he was not able to learn to read.

Conflict about curiosity may lead to insatiable learning in order to master anxiety, wanting to know more and more with an incessant unsatisfied feeling that still more must be learned. Some perpetual students are of this type. They do not have ordinary learning difficulties but they have a characterological inability to achieve completion, resolution, or to limit the scope of an assignment.

When learning becomes equated with sexual competition, education becomes stressful. The competition originally is with the parents, those who know more, and ideally this should be a spur to learning. But it may also involve anxiety: "I can never know as much as my mother or father," or, "If I try to know as much as my parents, I will surely fail," or "If I succeed in surpassing my father, I will be punished." These feelings arise out of fantasies which include hostile competitiveness toward and retaliation to the parents. From the anxiety comes inhibition in learning, or the need to fail, self-protective devices which end disadvantageously. Any of these unconscious equations of learning with sexuality can lead to the attitude that it is dangerous to succeed or that success is impossible and therefore there is no point in trying for success.

An adolescent boy whose father is a mathematician did well in every subject in school except mathematics. Testing revealed that he actually had good aptitude for this subject so that his family and teachers could not understand his poor performance in class and on examinations. In treatment it became apparent that the boy had unconscious anxiety over his competitive comparisons with his father. Out of oedipal fantasy he felt he could not be as successful as his father without incurring his father's wrath.

### LEARNING PROBLEMS ARISING OUT OF LATENCY PHASE OF DEVELOPMENT

Learning problems in latency can be related to conflict and developmental crises of earlier phases. Treatment requires understanding of these conflicts and crises which have intruded on the maturation of the learning process.

Latency is considered an ideal period for learning because earlier libidinal and aggressive impulses have by that time been subdued. Theoretically, previous conflicts have been resolved to attain an equilibrium and there is energy available for ego mastery that is neither sexual nor aggressive.

There are several mechanisms by means of which latency children learn. Learning by identification is important; the resolution of the oedipal and earlier conflicts takes place through identification with the parents. A child learns in order to be like the parental figure he admires and also because this loved parent wants him to learn.

Curiosity, which during the oedipal period is heavily invested in sexual drive, becomes neutralized in latency and is available for interest in the numerous fields of human knowledge and endeavor.

Although learning may still take place mainly for the purpose of pleasing the parent or the teacher, the latency child should begin to find satisfaction in pleasing himself, an indication that some internalization has taken place.

Superego learning continues in latency, that is, learning by following the rules, by memorizing, rote and repetition.

Many people continue in life learning by means of latency mechanisms exclusively and on the latency level.

## LEARNING PROBLEMS ARISING OUT OF ADOLESCENT PHASE OF DEVELOPMENT

Learning is an important issue in adolescence. Because of its ultimate use vocationally and for general adaptation to the adult world, education is a special task for adolescent integration. The way in which an adolescent adapts to learning may determine the course of his entire life. Postponement of solution to problems of learning is no longer possible because within the adolescent years important decisions must be made with far-reaching consequences. The adolescent should be able to begin learning for the acquisition of skills and the possession of knowledge. He should begin to develop the capacity for insight into the subject matter, the ability to make intellectual connections. But this mature kind of learning is not possible if the student is blocked by his own sexual and aggressive impulses.

Many adolescents continue to be motivated to learn only to please others. If, however, such an adolescent is progressing normally in school, the method, although immature, should not in itself be considered a problem. If he were to give up that motivation for learning before he developed others, the learning process might stop. When this kind of adolescent is in treatment for other problems frequently there is a period of time in which there may be failure to learn until the original problem is resolved which kept him from developing other and better motivations for learning. This type of learning problem can be dealt with more profitably in college where interruption of education is not as damaging as it is in high school. Students of varying ages attend colleges and it is possible to drop out of college for a year or more and return later; but the overage high school student is conspicuous enough to create social problems which may jeopardize completion of education.

A large proportion of the adolescents who are referred for treatment have learning problems. Under-achievement, even to the point of failure, occurs frequently in intellectually capable students. An important part of the problem is to determine how much of the personality is involved in learning and whether the adolescent sees learning as a meaningful task in terms of his own goals.

Frequently, although the necessity for and the desirability of education has been discussed by parents and teachers, the adolescent has not applied these values directly to himself; he feels aimless, without direction. It is important for him to see what he himself is striving for; the counselor needs to give the adolescent an understanding of his adolescent task. The focus in treatment with any adolescent is the integration of his personality and vocational aims are a part of this integration. Early in treatment an adolescent should be asked about his goals and directed or helped to think about them. When the extent of his involvement in learning has been understood, it is then possible to evaluate if the learning problem is an outcome of unresolved problems or conflicts of the past or simply a reaction to an immediate stress.

Adolescents should not be pushed into making premature vocational choices. But it is not necessary to formulate specific vocational goals early in high school in order to motivate adolescents toward general goals which tend to increase the investment in school and in education. Many high school students have never been asked to think about the kind of work they would like to do, how they might wish to earn a living, or enrich their leisure. Young adolescents often react favorably to the feeling that they are capable of making plans for the future. However vague the adolescent's formulation may be, it will give the counselor an opportunity to suggest the importance of appropriate educational background and training. High school, or the goal of college, then may become valuable for the adolescent's own purposes of attaining his ego ideal rather than remaining merely an imposed requirement.

One of the frequent and important causes of learning problems is displacement of hostile affects from the home to the school. This displacement may be conscious or unconscious. In treatment the adolescent is helped to recognize the displacement. Feelings should be directed to where they appropriately belong. It is not too difficult to achieve intellectual recognition, but this in itself is not enough. The next step is more difficult. The adolescent needs to be helped so that he is freer to accept the existence of hostility, to understand why and to feel the hostility.

A bright fifteen-year-old boy was a chronic nuisance to his teachers, disrespectful, sarcastic and argumentative. The history showed that this boy had been an aggressive feeder but chronically frustrated by a pervasively impatient mother. At home he became a model child, out of guilt displacing his hostility onto his female teachers. In treatment he easily recognized the displacement but refused to see that he was retaliating against his mother. However, even partial recognition brought about change in his actions toward his teachers; he began to get some satisfaction from the school work even without complete understanding of his hostile feelings.

After the adolescent has recognized the displacement, further steps depend on individual factors. If the parents are also in treatment and if they have the strength and the courage to endure it, the adolescent may be encouraged to express the hostility appropriately to them. Usually however, hostility may be dealt with within the treatment relationship itself by talking it out instead of acting it out. Some adolescents who are not able to bring anger out at home may express more or less subtle forms of hostility to the counselor. Often they may be openly hostile to the counselor and learn from the experience that their hostile feelings are not as lethal as they had feared.

Another approach in treatment is to appeal to the superego.

Mobilizing the adolescent's active sense of justice has the effect of creating guilt about the displacement. Most adolescents can accept that it is unfair to act hostilely to a teacher when the anger belongs elsewhere. By the discussion the counselor tacitly gives permission to the adolescent to express his anger at home or in the treatment session and hopes to help the adolescent contain his anger at school. The very process of discussion serves to abreact some of the anger; the process of evaluation and the intellectualization helps to neutralize the aggression.

Treatment of adolescent learning problems may be outlined as follows: elucidation of the problem; the development, minimally, of intellectual insight into the dynamics; the differentiation of school and teacher from home and parents; the opportunity for discussion of behavior as observed in treatment as well as elsewhere. At every phase the feelings are worked through with the goal in mind of the integration of the management of hostility. The adolescent must discover that learning should not be an arena for the battle between himself and his parents.

With some adolescents an effective technique is an appeal to their narcissism, enlisting the wish to function more successfully. The counselor lets the adolescent know that he has faith in the adolescent's intellectual capacities. He is assured that he has the intelligence also to understand his parents, to know why they act as they do and can acquire techniques for coping with them to their mutual advantage. This use of "psychology" makes the adolescent feel sophisticated and more adequate, and from this increased good feeling, better behavior may result.

As always when adolescents are in treatment the counselor must be alert to reality environmental factors and should be able to offer help in ameliorating disabling situations. By careful collaboration with the school changes may be arranged; skillful interpretation of the student's problem often helps the classroom teacher and the administration understand the causes of the difficulties and cope with them better. The school may punish classroom misbehavior by forbidding some pleasurable kinds of extracurricular activities when the student desperately needs the recognition and satisfaction of participation in dramatics or athletics. Frequently a teacher is relieved when she learns that hostility or rebellion is displaced rather than a reaction to her own personality. She need feel no personal sense of failure if a change to another teacher is indicated.

When the learning problems date back to early in the student's school career he may have missed acquiring some basic skills or information. Even if treatment succeeds in improving the student's patterns of learning he may be unable to keep up with high school classes unless the counselor arranges for tutoring in order to make up the previous gaps.

In treating adolescents, the counselor must be prepared for shifting issues; each one must be worked upon as it emerges. There is some danger with a guilty adolescent of a depression when he becomes aware of his own anger. With adolescents more acting out is to be expected at times in the course of treatment than with adults.

The relationship of the counselor to an adolescent is related in some ways to the qualities that make good teachers. When adults recall the best teacher they ever knew, they ordinarily remember a teacher who helped them, showed them the way out of some difficulty, had a special interest in them. People often say that a particular teacher affected the rest of their lives and remember with pleasure that this teacher communicated the feeling of interest or love. This communication of love is important for the counselor to convey. He should be able to diagnose the source of the adolescent's learning difficulty and, as a loving and giving substitute parent, create in the treatment situation new, more comfortable and successful methods of resolving the incapacitating conflicts.

# 14

# Characteristics of the
# Effective Counselor

THE MOST IMPORTANT tool of treatment with adolescents is the counselor himself. He offers himself as a source of gratification, as parent, friend, counselor, ego ideal, molder of superego. He uses himself in whatever role he needs to assume in order to repair the deficiencies in the adolescent's previous experience. Therefore the personality of the counselor becomes important. The ideal counselor does not exist but certain characteristics can be formulated that are necessary in order to work effectively with adolescents.

Many adults forget their own adolescence. In reaching integration they become defended against the adolescent conflicts. This process of defense makes many adults intolerant of adolescents and disturbed by them. The counselor who wants to be successful in the treatment of adolescents has to be aware of his own adolescent struggles and retain sympathetic understanding of the tasks that confront the adolescent personality. The ability to retain awareness relates to personality structure rather than to age. The good counselor has some access to his own inner life.

While retaining awareness of his adolescent conflicts, the counselor should have arrived at a tenable resolution of them.

He should have attained a reasonable degree of maturity. His reactions should be based on the needs of the individual adolescent with whom he is working, not on his own unconscious needs. A counselor still seriously involved in his own adolescence cannot work successfully with adolescents.

The counselor must be clear about his own values and maintain and uphold them. In this way he can help the adolescent to a realization of those standards which benefit him in his own environment. The adolescent must be prepared to live his own life, in his own setting, not the counselor's. The counselor does not condemn values different from his own merely because they are different but he emphasizes the necessity for attaining some set of standards. He is careful not to select issues for treatment on the basis of his own biases instead of on their intrinsic importance in the life of the adolescent.

A counselor should be a good source of identification for the adolescent, a potential source for gratification who can permit the positive longings of the adolescent to emerge. The adolescent needs a figure with whom to identify, whether as hero or ideal. The counselor should have the ability to form a good relationship with the adolescent, a positive rapport, which is wider in its scope than specific transferences.

The counselor must himself be a person of integrity in order to become an ego ideal for the adolescent. The present-day social order which condones or even encourages corruptions of one type or another places difficulties in the way of an adolescent who is working toward a mature superego of his own. Some part of the delinquent acting out of adolescents may have its base in their sensing of the lacunae in modern moral conduct; newspapers, television, motion pictures, and books are full of instances of vice glamorized and even rewarded. The adolescent sees that there are few absolute standards of right and wrong in the community and uses this observation to rationalize or justify his own behavior. The counselor should be able to counteract this tendency to moral equivocation, not in any punitive or moralizing manner but by being aware of the necessity for an adaptive set of values which allows for living with a minimum of guilt and anxiety. This does not imply that the counselor must attain the impossible goal of an entirely consistent superego of his own. He should be able to live comfortably with his own conscience. He should be aware of his own superego problems so that he is free to allow the adolescent to work out his problems in the way that is best suited to him.

Most young adolescents still retain their childlike superegos because they have not yet acquired worldly knowledge. A superego constitutes a problem only when it is extremely rigid, overstrict, or inadequate. A primary activity of the counselor is to help the adolescent develop an adequate superego and in order to do this the counselor must have an adequate superego of his own.

The counselor must like adolescents. It is not enough to have a special interest in working with adolescents. Liking is not the same as interest. The adolescent will sense and resent the kind of scientific interest that makes him an object for examination but he responds to genuine liking.

The counselor who likes adolescents will be able to become familiar with the adolescent's special language and activities, forming a bridge to the relationship. He does not have to have previous knowledge of the particular adolescent world any specific adolescent inhabits. He does not have to enter the adolescent world; he can always learn the meaning of a peculiar word usage or the current slang. Adolescents do not mind being questioned about their own vocabulary or activities if the question comes out of interest and concern, rather than ridicule or scorn. The counselor remains an adult in an adult world but he should be able to understand and accept the adolescent in his adolescent world.

The successful counselor requires a sense of balance, a light touch. Treatment with adolescents is a matter of walking on tiptoe, but in the way a dancer does, with assurance, not out of fear or anxiety. Humor is important but sarcasm is to be avoided. An adolescent cannot tolerate ridicule, and resents it it he thinks an adult is laughing at him. He will however enjoy having his counselor laugh with him. Heavy-handedness is fatal; delicate discernment is a prime attribute for the counselor who wants to work with adolescents.

The adults around an adolescent, his parents, or his teachers, frequently are heavily involved in the details and issues of daily life. The counselor avoids this kind of involvement. He is not over-concerned with bits of behavior, habits or activities which do not have grave or permanent importance. He keeps his perspective. He is serious when seriousness is necessary but handles lightly matters that are transitory and involve no weighty decisions. The length of a girl's skirts or a boy's hair may be focal points for family conflict but the counselor does not participate in these battles.

The adolescent's need for dignity is preserved by the counselor. He gets this across by the simple procedure of *listening* purposefully. An adult who genuinely listens is a new and flattering experience for most adolescents. They meet few adults who take them seriously; usually they are talked at and talked to. They respond avidly to an adult who pays them full attention. In contrast to most of the adults in their lives who are amused or intolerant, the counselor relates to the emerging adult in the adolescent rather than to the remnants of the child. By his manner, his speech and his body language, the counselor shows the adolescent that he believes in his capacity for adult functioning.

Tolerance and patience are useful characteristics for any counselor but it would not be possible to work with adolescents without large portions of these qualities. The counselor with adolescents must have the capacity to endure reverses and frustrations. The treatment process is slow and the counselor must learn to sit and wait without conveying to the adolescent dissatisfaction with the rate of progress.

Another useful ability is that of working collaboratively. The adolescent needs his counselor to help him with his parents, his school, perhaps a court or social agencies. The counselor must know how to help him effectively for the ultimate good of the adolescent and the community. This may at times involve considerable tact and diplomacy. The counselor must learn to withstand pressures from parents, teachers and community figures who may, in many instances, complain about the slow pace of treatment or about the "softness" of the counselor's attitude, mistaking for ineffectiveness the counselor's non-condemning tolerance for the adolescent.

Added to all those qualities is another which is necessary for counselors who work with adolescents. He must respect the parents of the adolescents he is treating. His deep interest in the adolescent and identification with him, may tend to make him feel negatively about parents. He must recognize that parents are complex personalities whose behavior is dictated by their own psychic structures. He knows that he needs the support and help of the parents of an adolescent for effective treatment and he does his best to enlist this aid. Parents will react to a negative attitude on the part of the counselor and out of this reaction may sabotage or even terminate treatment.

The physical characteristics of the counselor matter very little. He may be old or young, thin or fat, short or tall; he may or may not be good-looking; he may speak with a foreign or regional accent. The important factors are warmth, integrity and liking for the adolescent.

Adolescents will not be fooled. They can sniff out insincerity, phoniness, and sentimentality disguised as warmth. The wise counselor neither lies to an adolescent nor tries to pretend to him.

No two counselors can be alike. The fundamentals of treatment, the techniques, can be learned, but the same techniques, filtered through differing personalities, will be transmitted by the individual characteristics of the particular counselor. Style and flavor cannot be taught. Experience will increase the counselor's assurance in employing benignly the special characteristics that flow from his own personality.

# Selected Bibliography

Aichorn, A., *Wayward Youth,* The Viking Press, Inc., New York, 1948.

Ausubel, D. P., *Theory and Problems of Adolescent Development,* Grune and Stratton, New York, 1956.

Blos, P., *On Adolescence,* The Free Press of Glencoe, Inc., New York, 1960.

Erikson, E. H., "Identity and the Life Cycle," Monograph, *Psychological Issues,* Vol. I, No. 1, International Universities Press, Inc., New York, 1959.

Freud, A., "Adolescence," *Psychoanalytic Study of the Child,* Vol. XIII, International Universities Press, Inc., New York, 1958.

——, *Ego and the Mechanisms of Defense,* International Universities Press, Inc., New York, 1946.

Freud, S., *Three Essays on the Theory of Sexuality,* International Universities Press, Inc., New York, 1949.

Gitelson, M., "Character Synthesis: The Psychotherapeutic Problem of Adolescence," *American Journal of Orthopsychiatry,* Vol. XVIII (1948).

Group for Advancement of Psychiatry, *Normal Adolescence: Dynamics and Impact,* Charles Scribner's Sons, New York, 1968.

Hall, G. S., *Adolescence,* Appleton Co., New York, 1904.

Josselyn, I. M., *The Adolescent and His World,* Family Service Association of America, New York, 1952.

——, "The Ego in Adolescence," *American Journal of Orthopsychiatry,* Vol. XXIV (1954).

Lichter, S. O., Rapien, E. B., Seibert, F. M., and Sklansky, M. A., *The Drop-Outs*, The Free Press, A Division of the Macmillan Co., New York, 1962.

Offer, D., and Sabshin, M., *Normality: Theoretical and Clinical Concepts of Mental Health*, Basic Books, New York, 1966.

Sklansky, M. A., "Emotional Problems of Adolescence," *Emotional Problems of Children*, Lippincott Co., New York, 1958.

————, "Impulse Experience and Control in Adolescence," *Journal of American Academy of Child Psychiatry*, Vol. IV (1965).

Sklansky, M. A., and Lichter, S. O., "Some Observations on the Character of the Adolescent Ego," *The Social Service Review*, Vol. XXXI (1957).

Spiegel, L. A., "Review of Contributions to a Psychoanalytic Theory of Adolescence," *Psychoanalytic Study of the Child*, Vol. VI, International Universities Press, Inc., New York, 1951.

# Index